SACRED AND CONSTRUCTIVE

ART:

ITS ORIGIN AND PROGRESS.

A SERIES OF ESSAYS.

BY

CALVIN N. OTIS, Architect.

NEW YORK:
G. P. PUTNAM & SON.
1869.

STEREOTYPED BY
DENNIS BRO'S & CO.,
AUBURN, N. Y.

PRINTED BY
TROW & SMITH,
50 GREEN STREET, N. Y.

CONTENTS.

PREFACE.

In composing this work, it has not been my object merely to "write a book," but to place, if possible, before the public, in as clear and simple a form as practicable, the cause, origin, nature, and objects of Constructive Art.

While a student of Architecture, I became conscious of the public necessity of a work of this nature, and I have watched the progress of literature with some impatience, hoping the subject would attract the attention of some able and accomplished scholar.

As no work of a similar nature has yet appeared, and still impressed with the idea of its public necessity, I have ventured upon the undertaking, trusting that a generous public will attribute its imperfections to the author, and not to the subject—as I consider the subject one of the noblest yet unexplored by literature.

The work might have been made more clear, as well as more interesting, by a series of illustrations ; but that would have increased the expense beyond what I have felt justified in undertaking.

I have, consequently, endeavored to render the subject clear and comprehensible by letter-press alone. How far I have succeeded, I leave for a candid public to decide.

BUFFALO, December, 1867.

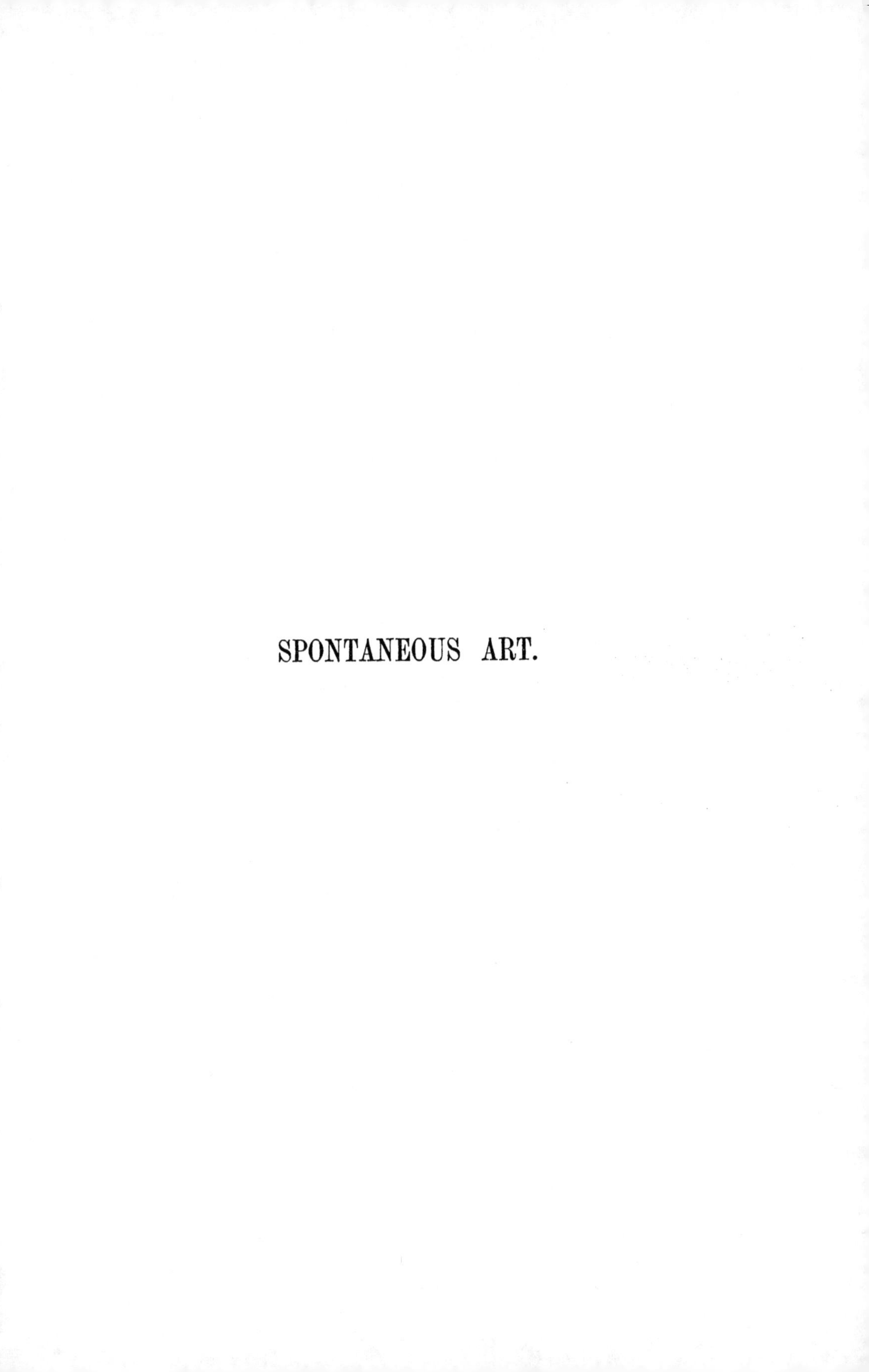

SPONTANEOUS ART.

SPONTANEOUS ART.

Is art a mere invention to satisfy physical necessity? or is it an outward manifestation of human impulse, hopes, and aspirations—the spontaneous outflow of sensuous emotion? If it be the former, then very little can be said upon the subject; but if it is conceded to be the latter, then its laws of development are coeval with, and coequal to, those which govern human progress and social development.

And since art has a significance only in delineating subjects and objects which are developed under some form of human organization, the history of its origin and development, therefore, is identical with that of civilization. Consequently, without a historic basis, the subject of art cannot be rationally treated; although it may be the product of the genius of individuals, yet its objects at all times are to delineate man as a social and moral being. Yet if it be conceded that art has its development in the growth of history, that makes it none the less ideal in its origin, nor none the less the product of true genius, since civilization is but the result of the aggregate labors of individual genius. What is history but the record of human action, thought, impulse, and aspiration? Conquest and subjugation, religion, government, art, science, literature, all emanate from the same source, human impulse, all existing simultaneously, either active or passive, and hence each has its influence in a greater or less degree upon every other.

In one era of history, religion reigns supreme, manifesting its ideal emotions and aspirations in poetic legends and in symbolic forms of art; in another era, it promulgates an ethical system as the basis of religious and political organizations, which give rise to discussion of the true relations of the governors to the governed; then to the relations of man to his Creator, which give rise to systems of philosophy, and thence lead to the investigation of the laws which govern created things, or to the development of the natural sciences.

In all these varied conditions of social development, art lends its aid to express and embody the ideal sentiment of the age; to create, beautify, and adorn whatever the necessities and desires of society may require. Nor is it to mere genius alone—in the artistic sense—that we are to attribute the achievement of human progress; but to each and all of the faculties conjointly which mankind possess.

Of these varied faculties and their differentiated qualities, we may not be able to strictly define their varied relations; yet their extremes are definable, and susceptible of delineation.

Sensuous emotion and non-sensuous reason are faculties common to every individual, varying, in each, in combination more than in quality.

Granted they are the extremes of human faculties; yet neither is competent to perform a great and useful work without the aid, in a greater or less degree, of the other. Hence, all mental action falls within these two extremes; and since there is no visible line of separation, their influences are ever commingled in ever-varying quantities. As these faculties are innate in the individual, one or the other will be the more prominent, in proportion as there is evidence of genius or talent in force of character; and as no two individuals are precisely the same in mental or physical organization, consequently mankind in the aggregate will ever vibrate between these two extremes.

Thus we have the theologic era, when sensuous emotion is in the ascendant, when God reveals himself immediately to consciousness, but not mediately through his works to non-sensuous reason. In this age, theology and politics are one; and poetry and art reign supreme in the intellectual world.

In the metaphysical age, religion assumes more definite forms, originates creeds, attempts to define the attributes of Deity, and to interpret the laws he has decreed for the moral government of the intelligent beings he has created. In this age, government assumes some definite form of despotism, monarchy, or republicanism, and art becomes utilized in the service of religious and social organizations.

In the philosophic age, religion assumes a more rational form; governments assume constitutional forms, defining the rights and duties of the governed and governors. Art ceases to be a passion, and declines into a condition of taste and refinement, or perhaps into mere fashion.

The scientific is the age of critical analysis. Religion divests itself of its outward forms of an ignorant age; philosophy resolves Deity into an infinite, creative power, a consistent and uniform law-maker; science investigates analytically and synthetically created Nature, to discover and to define the laws which govern and sustain its uniform order of movement. Critics analyze art, and discover it to be a compound of three equal parts—man, nature, necessity.

Having made this discovery, the learned quidnunc proceeds to define the laws which govern the development of art, and ascertains that they are governed by the rule of three; thus, as man is to nature, so is necessity to the object sought to be attained.

Says the critic of critics, You have not stated the subject correctly; the true theory is, as man is to necessity, so is nature to the object sought to be attained. But the professional artist, not clearly comprehending either proposition, proceeds with his labors in accordance with the dictates of his own genius.

Now, it is not claimed that the above mentioned eras of history ever had, or ever will have, that strictly-defined outline of development as herein described; but they are pointed out as the prominent features in the development of civilization; and, as will be seen hereafter, one element has been more active and prominent than others in certain periods of history.

The evolutions of intellectual, moral, and social progress does not imply a process of elimination of certain faculties, and the gradual creation of others to fill their places. The mental transition from the belief in fetichism to polytheism, and from polytheism to monotheism, does not imply so much a diminution of religious sentiment, as it implies a radical change in the ideal conceptions of the nature and attributes of Deity. Fetichism is the conception of the existence of a Deity, without attributing to him definite attributes; while monotheism is but a higher generalization of the imperfect conceptions of polytheism; that is, it is the conception of the existence of one God, to whom is attributed all the attributes that polytheism had conceived to belong to a plurality of gods.

Monotheism tends to the belief in general, more than in special laws; ascribes all phenomena to natural laws rather than to supernatural causes, which leads to the observation and study of natural phenomena to determine the laws that govern it. Yet so imperfect are the developments of these laws, that human impulse is still governed more by its instinctive belief, than by the accumulated facts of its experience. God still reveals himself immediately to consciousness. Consequently, religious impulse is as active an element under the regime of monotheism, as is philosophy or science.

It does appear that as humanity progresses, and higher developments of civilization are attained, labor assumes a more systematic form; each specialty is assigned to a particular class; which implies that progress is the bringing into immediate action the greater number and variety of human faculties.

Thus, under the regime of monotheism, the special province of theology is to guide and instruct the religious and moral world, philosophy the intellectual world, and politics and science the physical or material world. Yet these three elements of human economy are not entirely independent of each other, since they all aim to accomplish the same grand purpose—the moral and intellectual elevation of society.

Religious belief and philosophic thought are resolved into systems under uniform laws; politics rises to constitutional principles; and art is subjected to the purposes of utility, under the guidance of a genius of cultivated taste and refinement. Non-sensuous reason now divides the domain of intellectual action with sensuous emotion;

yet neither can ever wholly usurp it; for, since we can never attain to the absolute by aiming at higher generalities of the relative, consequently, Deity, God, Creator, Cause, will ever remain as so many convertible terms, vainly striving to express an "Eternal Mystery."

Nor is the essence of the Divine Being the only mystery man cannot solve: he cannot explain the mystery of his own consciousness; nor can he clearly explain why he reasons, except it is by impulse,—the manifestation of Divine inspiration in the soul.

Neither can we assign a reason why an individual produces a work of art, unless it is from impulse; and the reason why he is more of an artist than the mass of individuals is, that he has a stronger impulse in that direction, has a more sensitive organization, feels more acutely, and has a higher ideal conception of the beautiful and the sublime.

While the producing of works of art is entirely the labor of individuals, yet art has a significance only as it illustrates some subject and object immediately related to social organizations; when it becomes a symbolic language, expressive of the ideas, sentiments, and impulses of that particular age.

Clearly, then, the law of the development of art in any and every era of human history, is the embodiment of the leading ideas, sentiments, impulse, and passions of the age in symbolic forms. As the professional artist is ever a close observer of the age in which he lives, his sensitive organization becomes electrified with its sentiments and ideas; and by impulse he gives to them a visible and durable existence in symbolic forms.

We must also consider the egoism of man's nature, which is more apparent in art than in most other subjects, for the simple reason that it addresses itself to our finer sentiments and nobler impulses.

Man cannot conceive a Divine Being as possessing attributes which differ from his own, however he can conceive that Deity may possess infinite attributes; yet man cannot comprehend infinity.

Art is ever striving to personate Divinity, yet always represents him in the human form.

As the human form is the most beautiful and symmetrical object in created Nature, the artist makes it his especial study, for the two-fold purpose of comprehending forms of beauty, and their harmony of proportions.

But the life-spring of art is in the rhythm of the artist's emotions, where impulse is pregnant with the harmony of proportions, and the ideal conceptions overflow with forms of beauty. Yet it is not so much the mere impulse of the artist, as it is the genius and enthusiasm of humanity, which is ever creating, building, enlarging, and destroying. First led and swayed by sensuous emotion, it founds or conceives a religious system; poetry describes it in legends, and art illustrates its subjects and objects in symbolic forms; and as it progresses from era to era, is gradually transformed from the ideal to the actual; when non-sensuous reason assumes the control of mental action, philosophy takes precedence of poetry and art, iconoclasm destroys the legends of sensuous faith, and its organic system and its school of arts decline together. While the organic system may perish, yet its poetry and the spirit of its arts may be preserved as a valuable heritage, since they form a part of human history; developed under the influences of certain religious ideas, a record of man's efforts to attain the "true, beautiful, and good;" and if nothing of its spirit was preserved from the decline of its organic system in the effort to re-organize, man would commence at the original starting point; and hence the history of the past is the fulcrum on which the lever rests, that elevates society to a higher constitution of development or of civilization.

The gregarious nature of man necessitates organization; and organization necessitates structure; and infantile structure is measure and metre, in harmony with youthful impulse, aspirations, and desires.

Hence, the infancy of Nations, like the infancy of individuals, is sensuous, imaginative, credulous, hopeful, aspiring, and ever susceptible to new impressions.

This is clearly the poetic age of life; religion is electrified with the supernatural, Deity is occupied with the immediate supervision of the affairs of man, and all phenomena is caused by his special decrees.

Man dwells in a hallucination of sensuous emotion; he fancies Deity and man brought into immediate concert; makes Deity to decree that he shall do just what his impulse and desires prompt him to do; then falls down and worships him; arises, and erects a monument to commemorate the act, the time, and the place—and history is born, progress is inaugurated, the crusade against ignorance and barbarism is organized and put in motion, to achieve civilization.

Necessity and desire is ever stimulating faith, hope, and will, to try all forms and conditions of human life: first a Chaldee-Babylonian; then a superstitious and monotonous Egyptian; next a volatile, fickle, and vivacious Greek; then subsiding into the cold, calculating, ambitious, and tyrannical Roman; and finally relapsing into barbarism, to lay anew the foundations of the temple of God upon a broader, more elevated, more humane faith —that the temple may become more expansive, more elevated—that its portals may become the highway of all mankind.

Now, this may appear as a highly-wrought, fanciful, and purely imaginative picture, having no historic analogy; yet it is the thesis of this work; and the effort will be made in future chapters to produce its forms, shadows, and coloring from veritable history.

When man wills to act, and does act, it becomes a fact; and if a record is made of it, it thus passes into history, and of necessity becomes an object which will influence the thoughts and acts of coming generations, so long as the record continues an object of sight or of thought. Yet these external influences in no way changes the nature of man, but is a new and ever-varying influence; ever stimulating and awakening new and varied ideas and dormant faculties. Hence the eclecticism and greater variety and activity of the ever "progressive" civilization.

Let us not lay the "flattering unction to our

souls" that because the Ancient and Middle Age have lived, done their work, and passed off the stage of action, that we can borrow their livery, and sit down in ease and security. True, their mantle has fallen gently upon our shoulders; let us wear it with dignity and humility; but let us go "about our Master's business," since we have more work to perform than had the Ancient or Middle Age; for the reason we have a greater variety of work to perform. God is merciful to all men, but most merciful to those most deserving. There are greater blessings in store for those who labor earnestly and with a will, than for those who labor not at all.

All preceding ages have accomplished their destiny by adhering to their own faith, doing their work with a will, and thus achieving what necessity and desire aspired to attain.

Every era of history has its peculiar organization and order of development; yet function is perpetual; it never becomes a dogma; a perpetual vitality is the vital element of all and of every form of development.

In the infant development of organizations in America, function aimed not so much to develop the beautiful, as to discard dogmas that had grown up in ignorance, and perpetuated by despotism; and to lay broad and deep the foundations of liberal and humane institutions, resting upon Christian ethics.

In this effort, disintegration of an organized despotism was the first grand move, and that was inaugurated in Europe before emigration commenced to flow toward the Western Continent, and was there continued in the form of religious persecution, and the organization of new sects, separated Church and State, and secured religious freedom by separating the religious community into a variety of sects, while no one sect was able to secure supreme control; thus compelling all to the exercise of tolerance.

Religious liberty secured, political liberty was sure to follow; the revolution was essential to sever the political connections of the colonies from the mother country; that accomplished, and the federal constitution adopted, the organization of liberal and progressive institutions was achieved. Religious and political revolutions neither stimulate nor develop the higher elements of art, yet their necessities may stimulate the development of mechanical construction. The production of art is not the work of antagonisms, but of the unity and harmony of social organizations.

All such organizations have their own works to do, and their own special objects to accomplish, and whether they produce an original school of ornamentation, or imitate one already developed, adaptation to purpose must be the leading idea; and hence, construction must be primary, and ornamentation secondary, in all conditions of progressive development.

The invention of the alphabet was not the development of literature, but it was the discovery of the means essential to its development.

Neither was the Greek school of constructive art the development of a great system of construction; yet it was the development of a very complete system of ornamentation. The Romans developed a great system of construction, yet they imitated the Greek system of ornamentation, but modified to harmonize with their own peculiar wants and necessities.

And thus it has been with all schools since the Greeks, and thus it will continue to be. Each succeeding school grows out of the special wants and necessities of the age which produces it.

And thus it will be in our own country. If we study adaptation of plan to purpose as the primary law of design, we shall eventually develop the greatest school of constructive art the world has yet seen; for the simple reason that we have a greater number and variety of wants and necessities to supply, and hence there must be a more expansive constructive system, and, consequently, a more varied system of ornamentation.

No nation or people ever developed a high school of constructive art by seeking after novelties, or by straining at effect by excess of ornamentation; neither shall we achieve the "Excelsior" by merely aping to servilely imitate European schools.

Any mere imitator can exhaust the whole vocabulary of ornament upon a single structure, and yet not rise above the meretricious. Genius alone can design an edifice that in plan and construction shall be perfectly adapted to the use intended, and so ornament it that it shall clearly and pleasingly express the purpose for which it was designed. That is constructive art in its highest and truest sense.

In comparing modern with ancient constructive art, the most striking feature is the impermanency of the former as compared with the latter.

Without reflection, it might perhaps be thought that the higher development of civilization attained, the more permanent would be the structures required to serve its purposes. Yet such is not the fact, since the history of the rise and development of constructive art proves the reverse to be true; and in this, when carefully investigated, there is nothing very remarkable or incomprehensible. This will be more fully demonstrated in the investigation in future chapters; yet it is proper here to give a general outline of what will hereafter be shown more minutely in detail.

All barbarous races from time immemorial have recorded signal events at special localities, by heaping cairns of stone, or mounds of earth, and to this pre-organic class of structures belong the Egyptian pyramids.

The Egyptian temple embraced the structural organization known as the post and lintel system, that is, the setting of vertical posts, and placing a horizontal lintel, or beam, upon their ends. Its only element of development was the piling of mass upon mass.

Their social institutions were founded upon a sacerdotal despotism; every form and ceremony was stereotyped; consequently, all thought became chronic. Art did not rise far above mechanism; for the reason, Deity was an all-pervading essence, had no material form, nor distinctive attributes; consequently could not decree a system of laws to govern and control human action, and thus develop human reason upon a rational basis. The religious system of the Greeks was founded upon anthropomorphism; they not merely conceived Deity as possessing a corporeal form, with distinctive attributes, but believed in his immediate interposition in the affairs of man.

The human mind thus emancipated and elevated to the conception of a Deity possessing the same attributes as man, there were no limits to conception, emotion and reason, save the limits of human faculties.

Yet they did not conceive the existence of one Deity who possessed all the attributes which man possesses; but conceived the existence of a plurality of gods, each one possessing different attributes. Now, it would appear that the conception of a plurality of gods would naturally give rise to a greater variety in art, than the conception of a single Deity, possessing all the divine attributes.

Such, however, was not the fact, which simply proves that something more than the belief in anthropomorphism is essential to progress, or to the development of civilization, yet those essentials can only be delineated by the analysis of the history of progress itself.

Yet, from the nature of the case, we must view the history of the past from our present stand-point; we behold the results of their impulses and their acts in the monuments they erected; yet we can never have a clear conception of their emotions, impulses, and passions; in a word, mankind can never again be the Egyptians, Greeks, Romans, early or middle age Christians of the past.

The permanency of ancient monuments of art has its explanation in the unchangeableness of the institutions which produced them. All the energies of society were concentrated upon a single object, and hence their permanency. They had a beginning and an ending, but no growth or development and decline. This applies strictly to the Egyptian, but less true of the Greeks, and and still less true of the Romans. It may be said of Greek art, that it had an inception and development in a single direction, while Roman art had an inception and development in various directions, to serve various purposes, and hence its variety implies relative impermanency.

Yet this does not clearly explain the impermanency of modern as compared with ancient constructive art.

Take, as an illustration, the feudal castle of the Middle Age, which was the original prototype of our modern palaces, villas, and common dwellings.

Its origin was a fortified habitation for man and beast, consisting of a number of stories in height, and one or more apartments upon each story.

These massive, ill-lighted, and ill-ventilated structures served the purposes of a certain social condition; but as society progressed, they were modified, enlarged, or removed, as social necessities required.

In like manner, the Reformation has given a certain impermanency to ecclesiastical structures, which they did not possess when all Europe was Catholic.

This is owing to two causes: first, the religious world is no more a unit, but divided into a variety of sects, which weakens its moral force; and second, religious societies no longer control great wealth, which limits their means, and thus necessitates the erection of comparatively small and impermanent structures.

But what renders modern constructive art more

impermanent than all the other causes, is the varied, shifting, and changeable character of commerce.

The rapid growth and extension of modern commerce has built and re-built cities, and is still razing and re-building whole streets, squares, and blocks; nor will there be an end of it until commerce culminates and declines, where it now flourishes,—to rise up and flourish in other portions of the globe. Such, at least, is its past history; and it is rational to infer that such will be its future.

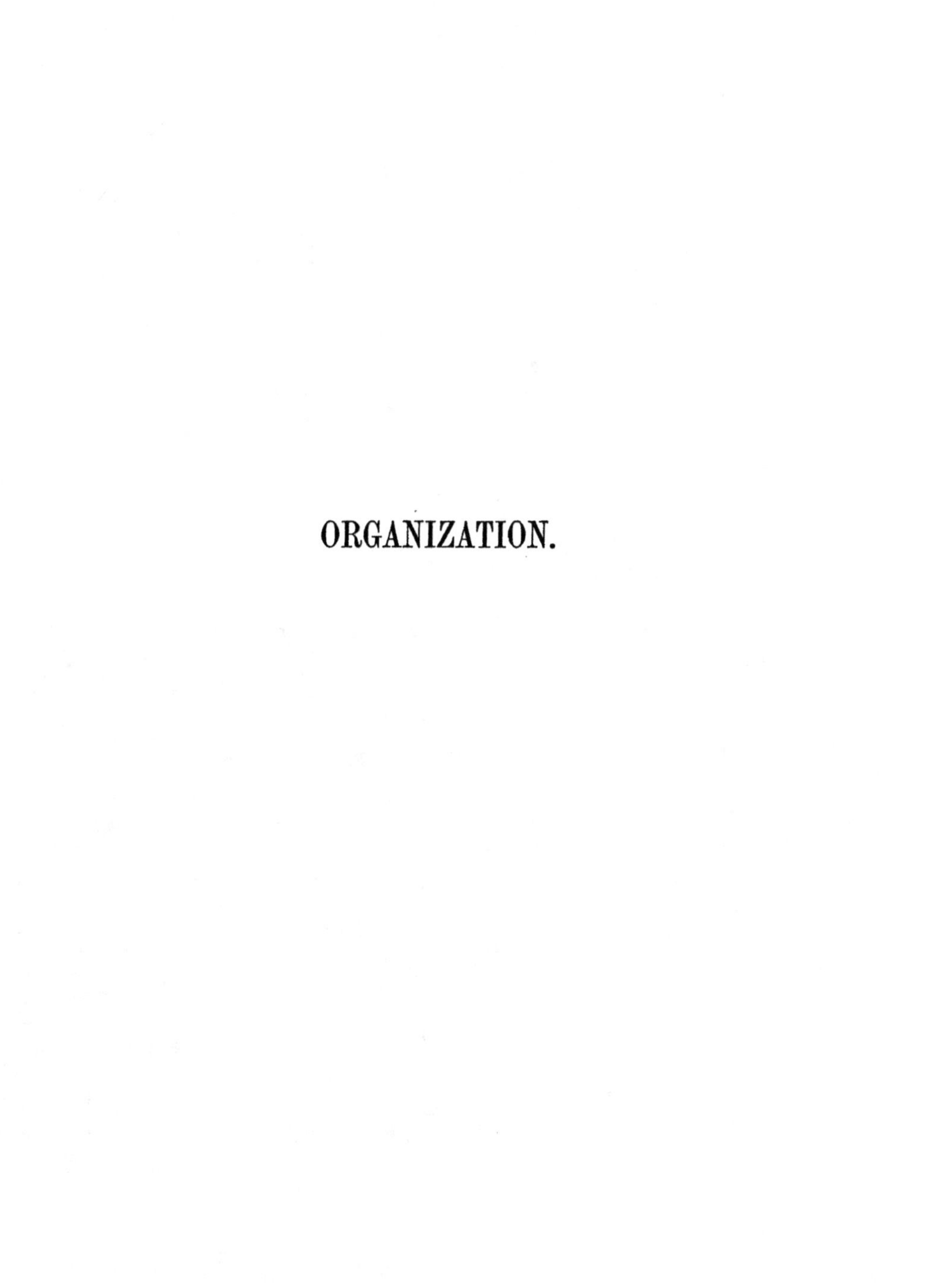

ORGANIZATION.

ORGANIZATION.

All human organizations, as well as all human productions, partake in a greater or less degree of the nature of man; and since he is but an individual organism, consequently, all social organizations are but the aggregation of indivi dual organisms. Societies organize to accomplish a purpose; the achievement of that purpose is the adoption and development of some moral or political principle which tends to the moral and intellectual elevation of society.

The organization of religious society is not the practical development of religious principles, but the discovery of the means essential to their development.

Nor is the adoption of a federal constitution the full realization of individual liberty, but it is the means essential to the guidance of the acts of governors and the governed; to protect the authority of the former, and also to secure the largest liberty of the latter; clearly, this can only be realized by practice, which simply means progressive development.

And thus, the simplest construction of any sort, for mere protection, which is to supply the earliest wants of an infant organization, may result in the development of a school of constructive art—construction to supply the physical necessities, and ornamentation to give expression to the moral and intellectual condition of society.

Yet there may be a condition of organization or aggregation without achieving progressive development; as, for instance, witness Chaldaic Babylonia, which appears, from what can be gathered of its scanty history, to have been little more than an immense aggregation of individuals, held together by the cohesive force of a single despotic will, aided by the quiet submission of the gregarious nature of man, in an ignorant or undeveloped state. So far as is known, they had no definite system of pronounced laws nor a strictly defined religious creed, but paid adoration to the sun and to fire as symbols of the "Mysterious and Great Unknown."

The conception of a mysterious power, without definite attributes, is but a fetich, and leads to the conception of no higher law than self-will; nor will it develop a higher mental state than mechanism. Such, at least, are the teachings of history. In the description of the city of Babylon, its walls and hanging gardens, there is ample evidence of a perfect knowledge of that system of construction which was developed in the use of bricks.

As Babylon stood upon the great alluvial plains which form the borders of the Euphrates, bricks were the only available materials for constructive purposes; and as they had no defined system of religion nor traditional history, there was nothing definite to symbolize; and hence they had no special use for materials for ornamentation. And yet there is ample evidence that the Babylonians were as familiar with the use of the arch as were the Romans, or modern workers in bricks.

The history of Babylon goes to prove that there may be construction without ornamentation, yet we have no evidence of ornamentation without construction, which may be interpreted to mean that there may be a body containing all the attributes which pertain to man, and yet but a moiety are in a vital developing state. Therefore, the art of ornamental construction is something quite different from mere building, as idealism is something quite different from materialism; and as the aspirations of the soul, is something quite different from the material wants of the body.

As animal life must precede mental development, in like manner construction must precede ornamentation, and so also must organization precede development. Organization, therefore, implies something more than mere aggregation; it implies the adoption of certain rules of action, which is to judge the outward acts of each and every individual composing the organization, or the adoption of certain religious creeds, to guide and control faith and hope in the development of intelligence and morality.

Now, to give a visible and durable outward expression of his internal sensuous emotions, man has invented certain forms and combination of forms, which were intended to express certain ideas, sentiments, attributes; and this external record of man's internal sentiments, thoughts, and emotions, is moral and intellectual development, or progressive civilization. These symbolic forms have been chiefly invented to express religious ideas, as that is a purely ideal subject, and the one in which the imagination takes its loftiest flights, and faith and hope conceive their noblest aspirations.

As man conceives Deity as possessing the same attributes as himself, for the simple reason, he cannot comprehend any others; so in inventing forms expressive of the divine attributes, he makes them to express that which is most pleasing to himself, in the belief that, in so doing, they will be the more acceptable to the Divine Being. In a general sense, those subjects and objects which excite our love, our admiration, and our veneration, are the themes which command the loftiest and noblest efforts of art, either plastic or constructive. And since all forms of art are symbolical, it can address itself only to intelligence and morality by personating attributes, as intelligence and morality can sympathize only with attributes.

Hence, anthropomorphism is the germ of ideal art, or of that form of art which personates attributes by such forms and colors as express certain ideas, acts, sentiments, passions, in place of merely imitating the forms and colors as presented in natural objects.

The Egyptian school presents the singular phenomena of a people expressing a belief in Deity, and having a form of worship, yet vainly striving to define his attributes; at one time taking the simple elements of nature as a symbol of Deity, such as animals and vegetables; at other times personating him in monstrosities, like the human body with the head of an animal, and the body of an animal with a human head.

There is a stiffness and stereotyped formality to their sculpture and constructive ornamentation, which does not indicate mental vivacity, or variety in ideal conceptions. Neither do their structures indicate a progressive development, since it is difficult to determine from construction or ornamentation which are their earlier, or which their later works.

There is also a similarity in their excavated tombs and their temples, both in form and decoration; and as their tombs are earlier works than their temples, it is more than probable the former suggested the form and mode of construction of the latter.

Their tombs consisted of a number of apartments of unequal size and height; and where the apartments were large, masses of rock were left for supports, arranged in the same manner as were the columns in the temples, where large apartments were covered with a roof. The simplest form of post and lintel construction, is to place two upright posts, and place a lintel upon their ends; to form an inclosure, place posts upon the four corners of a square, and place lintels upon their ends; to make this a protection from the elements, fill the spaces between the posts with a wall, and place a flat stone upon the lintels for a roof. This substantially embraces the stone type of construction; to inclose a space larger than can be spanned with a single stone, columns are used, thus overcoming space by multiplying the points of support.

The remarkable feature in Egyptian structures, is the immense size of some of the stone used in construction; there is nothing in their ornamentation that indicates a refined taste; nor a love for, or appreciation of the beautiful. That they were a religious people—even to bigotry—there is ample evidence; yet there was nothing in the ideal conceptions of their gods, nor in their religious organizations, that tended to elevate the people above a condition of ignorance and superstition; and hence their institutions were non-progressive, and reached comparatively but a partial condition of civilization.

Perhaps the aspects of nature in the valley of the Nile did not awaken in the mind the higher order of ideal sentiments, nor suggest objects of beauty; while the mild climate required little shelter or raiment for the body, and the spontaneous production of the soil required very lit tle labor to procure food, and hence the larger portion of their time was devoted to religious ceremonies, and in the construction of monuments consecrated to religion, and to the memory of their rulers. Hence, neither necessity nor desire stimulated the development of reason to the point that gives birth to philosophy, and also to the investigation of the laws of nature which developes the natural sciences.

Now, when we turn from the study of Egyptian art, and investigate the elements of Greek art, we perceive a great change in imagination, thought, feeling, and action. Deity has assumed a corporeal form, possessing distinct attributes, similar to those man possess, and hence the sympathy and affection between man and Deity. Greek genius revelled in ideal creations, pronounced his gods as feeling and acting in sympathy with himself. This gave distinctness to ideas, to desires, and to aspirations, which rapidly developed distinctness of forms in plastic and constructive art.

The primitive element in Greek constructive

art was Pelasgic—the primitive inhabitants of Greece, whose works consisted of massive stone walls, gateways, tombs, and other works of a useful nature. It does not appear that they were temple builders, or that they had any structures of a purely sacred character—unless their tombs be considered as sacred fanes.

It was not until after the conquest of the Pelasgi by a foreign race in a more advanced state of civilization, and until nearly four centuries of darkness had passed, after the conquest, that constructive art commenced to develop beauty of form and outline, and harmony of proportions.

Hero-worship appears to have been the stimulating cause of the origin and development of Greek art; but to give to it a definite object, as well as distinctness of form, Epic poetry had first to describe the person and the acts of the heroes it sought to immortalize.

From what source the Epic poets derived the ideas which they wove into their descriptive songs, it is difficult to conceive; unless it was from the traditions of the actual struggles and contests in the conquest of the Pelasgi by a foreign race, the amalgamation which finally formed the Hellenic or Greek nation.

Nor was it until after the rise of Lyric poetry, and until the poet gave expression in language to his own emotions, sympathies, and aspirations, did the artist essay to give outward expression to his internal ideal conceptions in symbolic forms of beauty.

The Greeks were an imaginative, vivacious, and volatile people, fond of indulging in all manly sports; and to their national games may be attributed the cause of the origin and development of their school of sculpture.

The preparation for, and the participation in these games, developed the most perfect physical forms, and those forms the sculptor had for his models, as it was the custom to erect a statue in the forum in honor of the victor. And from these studies the artist drew his loftiest conceptions of the gigantic form and manly beauty of his hero god; and it is rational to suppose that the architect, in designing the monument that was to commemorate his heroic deeds, derived his ideas of the laws of harmony and proportions from the same source.

The Greek school of art may with propriety be classed as the school of physical beauty, from the fact that its special objects were to delineate physical action.

If we accept the above classification of the Greek school, we in a measure account for the universal admiration which it receives wherever it has been known, from the fact that the standard of physical beauty is substantially the same among all civilized nations.

The object of a Greek temple was, to receive within, the statue of the hero to whom the temple was dedicated ; while upon the exterior were sculptured the symbols expressive of his heroic deeds, all expressing physical action.

And as the forms and proportions of the body of the temple were made to harmonize with the sculpture, its massive columns, entablature, and pediments, were formed to express physical strength, dignity, and repose.

The completeness of the form of the temple structure goes to prove that its hero had achieved the full object of his mission, that the legends of his life and acts were a complete subject, having no immediate relation to any other. He was a self-sustaining individuality, and his temple was complete when it contained a full record of his life and acts.

So far as mere construction was concerned, the Greeks may have borrowed the post and lintel system of construction from the Egyptians, yet there was very little similarity of form, or of appearance, in the Egyptian and Greek temples; the former had no pediments, and seldom columns upon the exterior; while the latter were always crowned with pediments, had always columns front and rear, and frequently the cell of the temple was surrounded with a colonnade.

With a single exception, all the known Greek temples were symmetrical, the plan a rectangle parallelogram, all parts of equal heighth, and covered with a single roof. The form of the Greek temple was as original as was the Egyptian; and their symmetry of outline, harmony of proportions, and beauty of ornamentation, far surpassed the Egyptian, or any known school, before or since its development.

Yet it does appear that Greek genius exhausted itself upon the development of a single class of structures. With the exception of the Propylæa and a few monuments, there are no purely Greek structures known to us, except temples. It appears that neither municipal governments, agriculture, manufactures, nor commerce were developed to the point where they require certain structures for their special accommodation.

The Roman school had its inception in the useful more than in the ideal; they constructed bridges, sewers, wharves, and military roads, centuries before they erected edifices of any architectural pretensions. They learned of the Etruscans construction, which was a compound system of stone and bricks, used in the same structure. The Romans also learned of the Etruscans the use of the arch, which eventually became a very prominent feature in their school as an element of construction, and, finally, as a grand feature in their system of ornamentation.

The unimaginative and material nature of the Roman mind led their great abilities to aspire to universal conquest, more than to the study and practice of the arts. Consequently, they developed a system of construction long before any system of ornamentation was brought into general use. The sequel will show that there was nothing purely esthetical, or of a spontaneous nature, in the Roman school, but its development was in the gratification of sensual appetites.

The Romans were by nature great mechanics, but indifferent artists; and hence the possession of wealth, with the aid of foreign artists, was the cause of the development of their school of constructive art. This accounts for the fact that they produced no works of a high artistic merit until near the close of the Republic.

During the third century of the Empire, pagan genius culminated under the patronage of the Romans, and finally perished in debauchery. The fires upon her altars had expired, and public faith was dead. Hence, the timely advent of Christ, and the rapid spread of his doctrines. Yet it was many centuries after Christianity was proclaimed and accepted as the religion of the State, before it developed an original school of art. Nor is this very remarkable, when we consider the fact that at the advent, pagan genius was at its zenith; and although its decline was rapid, yet in the nature of the two systems of religion, and since they occupied the same territories, pagan esthetics must decline before Christian esthetics could develop, as there cannot exist two suns in the same firmament. And the cause of this was the great fact that Christianity addressed itself to the soul, the mind; while paganism had chiefly occupied itself with the beauty of, and the material wants of the body.

This distinction in sentiment, or religious impulse, gave rise to two distinct systems of esthetics; one led to the erection of structures, chiefly for external effect; and the other to the erection of structures, chiefly for internal use. It is a much easier task to describe the difference in structure and ornament of two radically different schools of constructive art, than it is to point out the causes why they were so radically different, since they both were the works of the same race of men. Yet it does appear the difference was caused by the difference in religious sentiment; difference in faith, in hope, and in action. As the temple was gradually transformed into a Christian church, its lines were extended to enlarge the interior space; windows were inserted into the walls to admit the light of heaven; more height was given to the structure, as its area was enlarged, and every modification tended more to vertical, and less to horizontal lines; and Christian art finally emancipated itself from pagan influence, and developed a school of Christian art by the construction of the pointed cathedrals of Central and Western Europe.

Now, this transition was merely to supply the wants and the necessities of Christian worship, and in accomplishing that end, developed a new system of construction. In the infancy of the Christian Church, constructive ornamentation was merely imitations of Roman and classic ornaments, which continued to decline in spirit of design and execution, until the Church had completed the organization of its hierarchy, adopted a ritual, and enforced a uniform discipline, which centralized thought, and bent the energies and passions of faith, hope, and action, in a single direction.

Yet the Christian constructive art has never fully emancipated itself from pagan influence in those localities where pagan art once flourished. Italy cannot boast of a single specimen of pure pointed constructive art, such as Germany, France, Spain, and the British Islands possess.

Pointed constructive art was the product of those Christianized Germanic tribes which peopled Western Europe. They were strangers to any form of civilization prior to their conversion to Christianity, and hence the originality of their school of constructive art, and hence, also, the propriety of the term, Pointed Christian Art.

When the discipline of the Church had brought law and order out of chaos, and gradually established systematic industry, towns were gradually built up, parishes organized, and church edifices erected, adapted to the wants of the occasion, and ornamented to express the poetic sentiment of their faith.

The pointed cathedrals of Western Europe are as purely Christian in their origin, as were Greek and Roman temples purely pagan; for the simple reason, the Christians were as sincere, as much in earnest, and as free from foreign influences, as were the Greeks or Romans.

In tracing more minutely hereafter the development of the two great systems, the cause and the necessity of the difference in construction and ornamentation will become more clear.

In contrasting the different schools of art, as well as different eras of history, it appears mankind have never discovered or invented but one system of geometry, nor but one system of mathematics.

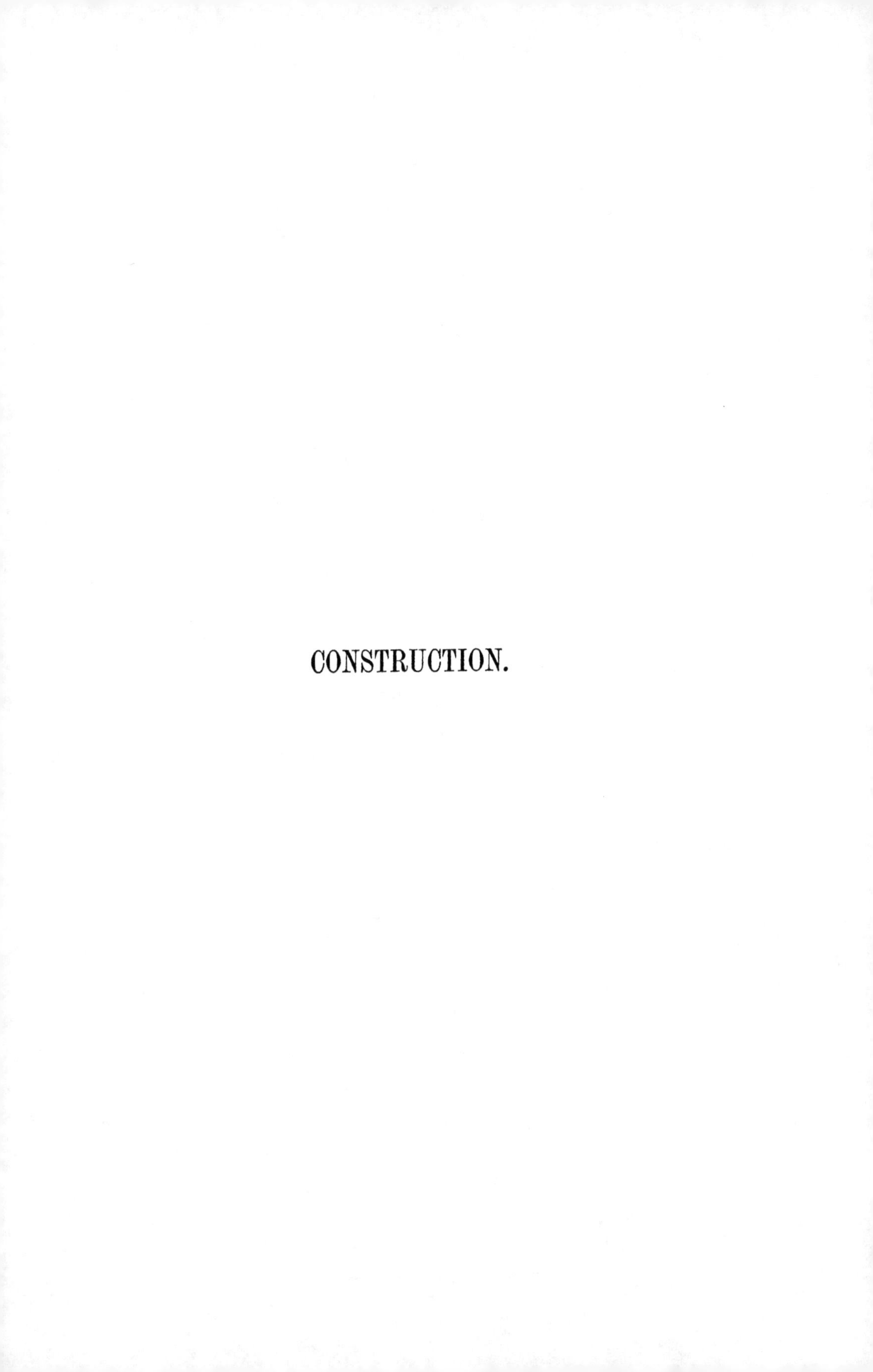

CONSTRUCTION.

CONSTRUCTION.

Although mankind have in different portions of the globe used different kinds of materials in constructing their various edifices, yet this is doubtless owing to the facility with which certain materials are procured, and to the influence of climate, more than to any radical difference in physical organization or modes of thought. The desire or necessity for building is common to mankind under all social organizations; and, consequently, the peculiar character of the organizations will determine the special objects of the structures. But the nature of the climate and the kinds of materials used, will doubtless control the peculiar mode of construction; and so long as the structures have no higher objects than protection from the elements, the kind of materials used, or the mode of using them, does not become important. When, however, the artistic element is introduced to give a certain expression of purpose to the structure, then certain forms must be introduced; and, consequently, certain kinds of materials become a matter of importance. If a high degree of artistic expression be sought, then the materials used will have a decided influence upon the mode of construction, and indirectly an influence upon the organizations of society. For structures of some form are essential to a civilized state, since they become the common centers around which all organizations are formed. When, however, organizations are formed, some special object is sought, or idea governs; the combination of construction and ornamentation is made to express those leading ideas; and hence the incipient organization of a school of art by the crystalization of certain ideas into symbolic forms. This development of a specialty by the combination of the two original elements, does not in any manner change the nature of those elements, but illustrates the mode of using them to accomplish a specific purpose. Therefore, the more schools of art there are developed, the more will the area of art be enlarged; since the resources of the two original elements are limited only by the organizations of society, and the mental and physical resources of man.

Of all the questions that have arisen in the investigation of various modes of construction, none have elicited such wide and varied views as the question of the origin of the arch.

From all the facts that can be gleaned from history, I am forced to the conclusion that the origin of the arch is to be sought, and found, in the physical necessities of man—the source from whence spring all useful inventions. The supposition that a people must be far advanced in civilization to bring the arch into use as an element of construction, I think is erroneous.

The only argument that can be urged in favor of its use, is convenience; that it is a higher element of beauty than the straight lintel, -when considered abstractly,–is a point upon which mankind will differ, under different external influences. This is no mere assumption, as the evidences of history fully sustain my position.

It is not possible for man to judge correctly of the motives or resources of man, with thousands of years intervening; but if we take as evidence the records of his past history, his resources have ever been adequate to the demands made upon them.

Therefore, it is rational to suppose, that whenever man has arrived at that state where his religious and political organizations have required buildings of a certain character, his genius has never failed to supply them. But it is equally true that the constructive features of those edifices have uniformly been governed by climate, and the nature of the materials available for their construction. It is not my purpose to inquire into the causes which have decided the choice of materials, but to examine into the mode of using various kinds of materials. There are three distinct types of constructive art, namely, the wood type, the brick type, and the stone type; and, in my humble judgment, had their origin in the order they have been named.

If we examine with care the specimens of Asiatic

art, as shown in Mr. Fergusson's "Illustrated Hand Book of Architecture," we shall find the wood type among the Mongol race, especially in China, some portion of Hindu, and in Assyria. Their early specimens of constructive art, have the features of the wood type of construction.

The Persian school appears to have been a mixed or transition school, as its features exhibit the wood type, and also certain features of the stone type.

If we take history for our guide, the Chaldaic race produced the brick type, and, consequently, were the first to use the arch as an element in construction.

From the descriptions of the walls and other structures of the city of Babylon, by Herodotus, we are to infer, they were constructed of bricks. He says "the walls that inclosed the city were 87 feet thick and 350 feet high, constructed entirely of bricks—with 100 gateways, with brass gates." "The palaces of the Kings were situated on either side of the river Euphrates, and were joined by a bridge, and subterranean passage. The bridge may have been constructed of wood, but the subterranean passage could not with safety have been of wood. But his description of the hanging gardens are more explicit. "They were 400 feet square, raised upon terraces one above another, to the required height, and supported upon piers and a kind of vaulting; and the whole held together by a wall 20 feet thick." Now, if we receive this account as authentic, there is very little room for doubt as to who were the first to use the arch as an element in construction.

If Herodotus did not actually see in Babylon what he described, I am at a loss to conceive from what source he derived his ideas; since such works were then unknown to Greeks or Romans, nor was that system of construction then practiced by the Egyptians. We have, as further evidence, the description of Mr. Layard, of a vaulted chamber found in the ruins of Nineveh. He says "it was about 10 feet high, and the same in width. The arch was constructed upon the well-known principles of vaulted roofs, the bricks having been placed sideways, one against the other, and probably sustained by a frame-work until the vault was covered."

Mr. Layard's description of Nineveh proves their principal building material to have been sun-dried bricks, laid without cements.

Stone was used for ornamental purposes, and for tablets of record. No remains of columns were found in Nineveh; and if any were used, they were probably of wood. Such structures, as described by Mr. Layard, must have been roofed with wood; and he also states that the representations of palaces and other edifices discovered in their sculptures, represent flat roofs. The forms of roofs in Nineveh were the same as in Egypt, although Egyptian structures were wholly of stone; the climate in either case, doubtless, had more to do with the form, than the materials used in construction.

The intercourse between Assyria and Eygpt commenced as early as 1500 years before our era, and continued, at intervals at least, until the conquest of Egypt by Cambyses, about five hundred and twenty years before Christ; which may account for the appearance of the arch in certain Egyptian structures, of which so much has been written and so little proven in support of the theory that the Egyptians were the originators of the arch. It is not rational to suppose that the Egyptians, or any people, were the originators of so important an element in construction as the arch, and yet have made so little use of it as the Egyptians did. The arch was not an element of common use in construction, either in Egypt or Greece, prior to their conquest by the Romans; and if it occasionally appears anterior to that period, it must be considered as an exotic.

The question very naturally arises, How came the Romans by a knowledge of the arch, since they were not an inventive people? To satisfactorily solve this question, is the grand object of this chapter.

That the Romans obtained the first rudiments of their arts from the Etruscans, is now generally conceded; and it is also known that they possessed a knowledge of the arch almost from the founding of the city—a knowledge which they must have obtained from the Etruscans, or must have invented it. Who, then, were the Etruscans? and how came they by a knowledge of the arch, since they have left so few monuments to perpetuate their achievements in either arts or sciences? If we concede the Lydian origin of the Etruscans, it is not difficult to account for their knowledge of the arch. Now, as the Lydians were a branch of that Assyrian race that once inhabited the alluvial plains upon the borders of the Euphrates and Tigris, and as I have assumed that those people were workers in brick, and consequently familiar with the use of the arch, I also assume that the Lydians were also familiar with it when they passed into Italy, conquered, and amalgamated with the Pelasgi, and thus formed the Etruscan nation.

It is not, however, with the origin of the Etruscans that we have to do at present, only so far as relates to the use of the arch; and if we do not concede that they derived the knowledge of its use from Asia, we must then give them the credit of its invention, for it is now clearly established that they were the first to use it in Europe, in the concentric form. The Pelasgi were familiar with its use in the horizontal mode, but they were workers in stone, while the Lydians were workers in brick, and the union of the modes of construction developed the complete and free use of the arch as an element of construction, either in brick or stone.

The walls of some of the Etruscan cities were constructed of part stone and part brick—a mode of construction common with the Romans at a later period. The Etruscans were also familiar with the manufacture of terra-cotta, as the cinerary urns and other utensils found in their tombs clearly prove.

Now, if we set aside the theory of the Asiatic origin of the Etruscans, we have still in their works the evidence of the use of the arch in the concentric mode. Nor can I see any plausible reasons why the Etruscans would not have been as likely to have originated the arts, as the Egyptians or the Greeks, if in the nature of their structures it became the most convenient mode of construction.

If we admit there be such a thing as the architecture of nature, who is prepared to prove which is the rule, and which the exception—the post and lintel, or the pier and arch system of construction? Both have been practiced by prominent nations, and both are in use at the present day.

The pier and arch is a general system, while the post and lintel was subjective in its origin to a symbolized religion; its specific object was, personating the attributes of special deities, or hero gods, thus embodying, in symbolic forms, the poetic ideas of a people under certain peculiar mental and physical influences. And hence the post and lintel system originated in expressing certain ideas by means of certain forms and proportions; while the pier and arch system originated in the efforts to accomplish a purpose, without reference to any special poetic sentiment, and hence assumed its forms more from accident than design, was controlled by the physical necessities of climate and the nature of materials at command.

That constructive art owes to the post and lintel system its forms of beauty, and ideal laws of proportion, every one familiar with the subject must concede; but that it is indebted to the same system for those elastic elements of construction which it has acquired in modern practice, is quite a different matter. It is true, constructive art has derived from the post and lintel system that art language in the use of which the artist is enabled to impart an intelligible expression of purpose to his works; and it is also indebted to the pier and arch system for that elastic element in construction which renders it applicable to an infinite variety of purposes.

The post and lintel system gave distinctness and significance to forms, and fixed laws to proportions; and in doing this, limited their application to purpose without radical modification; but the substitution of the arch in place of the straight lintel, wrought such radical changes in construction, ornamentation, and proportions, which rendered it applicable to an infinite variety of purposes.

While constructive art still has its power of expression of purpose, by the use of forms which were developed in temple building, it has also acquired, by the adoption of the pier and arch mode of construction, other and quite different expressions by its application to different purposes. The Greek temple, however, still holds the first rank as an ideal form of beauty; for the simple reason, in their inception and development they had no other or higher objects to achieve; consequently, they will ever remain the standard of esthetics in constructive art.

But with the progress of civilization, and the present eclectic state of society, constructive art can no longer conform to the arbitrary laws of forms of beauty, and laws of proportion, as developed and established in the temple school; for the simple reason, another element of equal importance with that of abstract beauty has now to be considered; namely, utility, and judicious application of style to purpose and locality.

This new element of art has changed its primary objects from that of external effect, mainly, to that of internal use, chiefly. Without the aid of the arch, the building art could not have attained to such varied purposes as modern constructive art has achieved.

Therefore, it must be admitted, the pier and arch is the more general system than the post and lintel; for the reason, its adaptation may be almost universal; whereas the post and lintel style has rarely been successful, except when applied to the temple form. Temple building was the development of art as a specialty; and a school thus developed, may have its own special laws of proportion, which cannot be readily applied to another school with the same happy effect. Now, as there have been two distinct schools of constructive art developed upon two radically different systems of construction, the question of a universal, or natural law of art, is no longer to be entertained; its laws are universal, in the same sense as are those which govern the progress and development of social systems; their developments are simultaneous.

It is a question, however, how far art is subject to distinct laws, when developed as a specialty.

It is not my special object to discuss theories of

the development of art, as those are questions for philosophy to settle—since the same causes which produce art, also determine the laws of its development.

One assertion, however, I venture to make, and that is: those who create or produce works of art, are rarely in search of theories; while ambitious amateurs, who affect to be its special patrons, are ever ready to aid it with this gratuitous service.

If there were no other evidence than the two great schools of pagan and Christian art, there would be in their development sufficient evidence to prove the post and lintel system to be applicable to buildings of the temple form only with happy effect, while the pier and arch system is applicable to almost any form or outline of plan.

Now, as to whether man would use the arch as a principle in construction, before he had learned to express his ideal conceptions in symbolic forms, is a question to be settled, before it can be definitely determined as to whether the post and lintel system naturally precedes the pier and arch system; and in establishing this fact, will determine whether the origin of the arch might or might not have been anterior to the origin of Egyptian or of Greek art, or whether it might not have originated with those people who first had occasion to use it. The abstract question, Would man naturally use the post and lintel before he would the pier and arch? is one that pertains to the science of physiology more than to art; and since there is no positive evidence upon the subject, I assume the arch pertains to the science of construction more than to the art of ornamentation, and may be used as an element in construction, in the absence of all artistic sentiment; and hence, in its origin, would be as likely to precede as to follow it. It is not assumed that the development of a school of ornamentation controls its principles of construction, but rather adapts itself to it.

This is beautifully illustrated in the pointed cathedrals of Europe, as contrasted with the pagan temples.

It is almost surprising, when we reflect how few forms of geometry there are applicable to constructive art; and also, when we consider that the same forms were used in the pagan temples and Christian cathedrals, and yet witness the marked contrast in expression.

This marked difference in expression is perhaps as much owing to difference in elements of construction, as to difference in spirit of ornamentation.

The progress of society is constantly varying and enlarging the field of construction; and to this fact must be attributed the cause of the progress and development of art generally; and to the deterioration and disintegration of society, and consequent disorganization of thought, may be attributed its decline.

The practice of constructing buildings without embracing the ornamentation in the construction, is true art, in the same sense as would be the composition of a poem without regard to sentiment, and then insert the sentiment in the process of printing. It is clear, such practices cannot produce a high order of art; for the reason, they cannot give a proper expression of fitness of purpose.

Therefore, when construction and ornamentation are not interwoven into subject and object, the work will oftener be a failure than a success; and if it should be a success, it would be more from accident than from the application of true principles of art.

With the variety and amount of labor imposed upon man as a civilized being, we can attribute to each what he performs merely, yet not all that we may conceive he may have the ability to perform; for the ability to do, and the doing, are quite different things. Neither are we to assume that because a certain school of art attained to great perfection by the aid of certain influences, that all schools are necessarily inferior, that may vary from it in form or decoration. Under such an assumption, art is confined to mere imitation, assumes a chronic state, as there can be no further progress or development.

Fortunately for the progress of art, every true artist has conceived a different view of the subject; and while they admit the classic schools as the source from whence they derive their knowledge of forms and proportions, yet it is not the substance, but the spirit, they imitate; for the mere body of every constructive school of art, like the institutions which produced it, must culminate and decline, while its spirit will live as long as its monuments exist.

That light of heaven which inspires the hopes, and elevates the desires of man, ever flows from the same pure fountain; and if it falls upon a variety of soil, there will, doubtless, be a variety in the form and color of the fruit, and yet it may all be equally natural, and therefore all legitimate.

Who is prepared to assert that the soul of the Greek was not as fervent, as noble in its aspirations, when he conceived and produced his temples, as was that of the Christian when he conceived and produced his middle age cathedrals? The difference in these two schools is doubtless owing as much to the difference in the physical and mental condition of man, at the different eras in which the two schools were produced, as in the different sentiment of inspiration.

It is from inspiration that art emanates; and as man is the subject inspired, art flows from himself, and, consequently, is a counterpart of his physical and mental condition. What the perfect type of man is, or ought to be, is quite another matter; but when he achieves perfection, we may be assured art will have attained to an equally perfect state.

And now, are we to suppose that it is to the inventive genius of some obscure Egyptian or Greek,—and while in conflict with the spirit of his national art,—that the world is indebted for that noblest of architectural elements, the arch? Is any mind so credulous as to suppose that had the Egyptian or Greek never made the discovery,—and it is more than doubtful that he did,—there never would have been developed that noblest production of human genius, the Christian middle age art,—for what would that school have been without the use of the arch? What other constructive element could have been brought into use, that could have produced those lofty and expansive naves, choirs, aisles, and transepts, of the pointed cathedrals? Think you, that had not pagan genius bequeathed to humanity this noblest of all artistic elements, that Christianity would have been robbed of its birth-right? Not so. In the broad plains of Asia, before man ever "bowed the knee to Baal," the arch had been used as a constructive element; and when the human mind became again free from the influence of a symbolized religion, this universal element was again brought into use, not merely as an element of construction, but as the grand element of construction and ornamentation. The star of pagan genius could serve as a guide in its own meridian; but the light of heaven is the only universal light, and the source from whence all minor lights are reflected. Finally, the arch is a natural element in construction, and would as likely originate in China, India, Europe, as in Egypt or Greece, if, in the process of building, the nature of the materials used, and the character of the structure, required the use of it; for the genius of man calls into immediate action those elements only which its present necessities require.

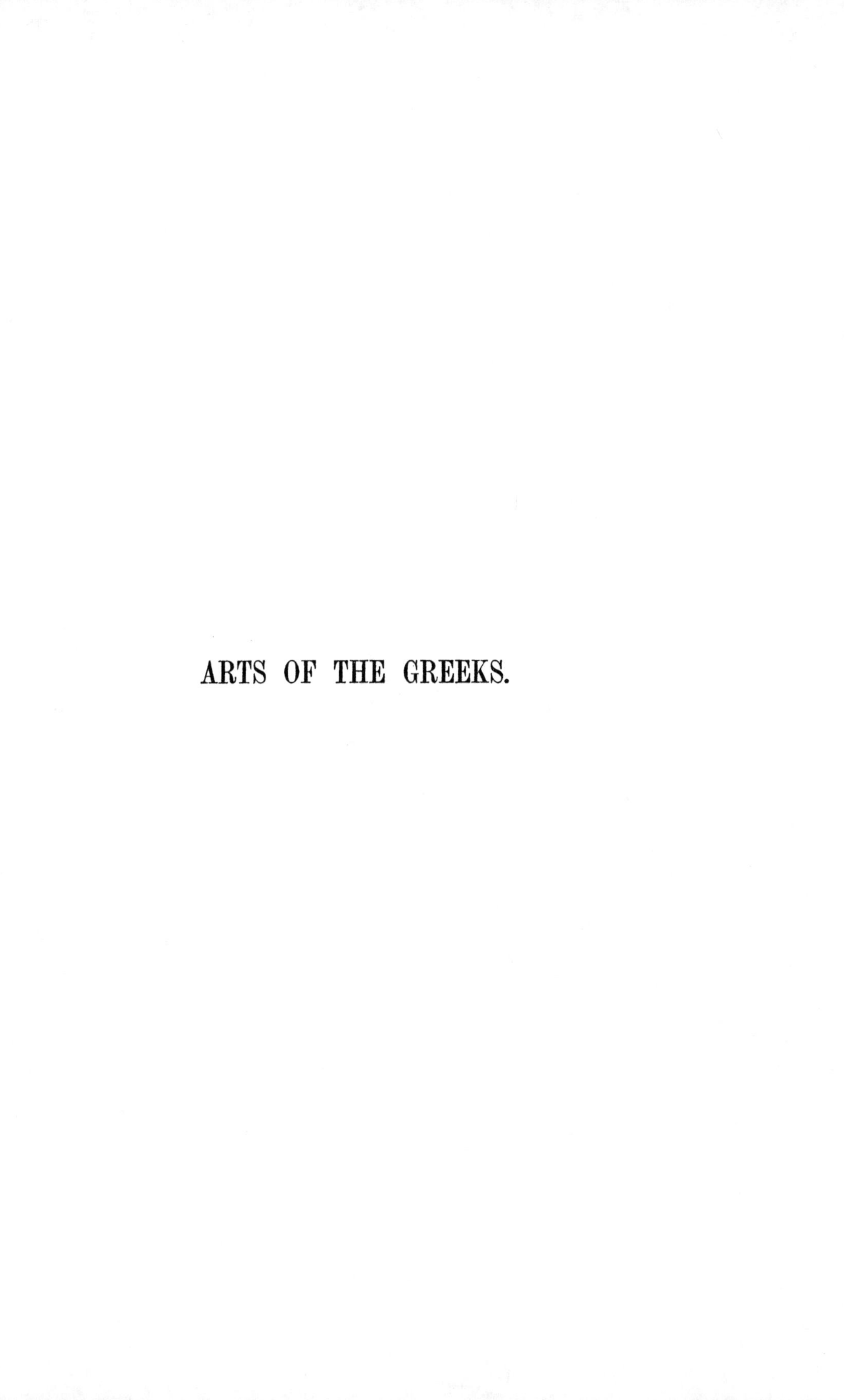

ARTS OF THE GREEKS.

ARTS OF THE GREEKS.

WHAT shall be said of the mythical age of Greek history? Because there are not sufficient records extant to prove their actuality, shall we assume they are a myth? Does not, rather, their very exaggeration of human attributes and action prove their identity with some enacted but unwritten history, which, having been transmitted traditionally for generations, became more vague and indistinct the further it receded, until it assumed its mythical form.

That mankind existed upon the earth for indefinite ages prior to the birth of history, no sane mind can doubt; yet it must be admitted they could not have existed in a civilized state, since civilization implies an enacted and written history. And since the primary laws of human life do not necessarily imply a civilized state, and as all states of existence are conditioned by some law; therefore, civilization must be the result of the development of those secondary laws which are only manifest in guiding human progress.

Therefore, civilization is not achieved by the gradual growth of new attributes or elements in man, but by the unfolding and expansion of his primitive nature. Yet these primitive elements may remain dormant and inactive, and man still continue to exist, surrounded by the phenomena of nature. Therefore, climate, soil, and the aspects of nature, are not the only elements which induce civilization.

Consequently, civilization is but another name for human progress, or the development of man's inner nature, which is never wholly conditioned in any one individual, generation, or nation, but is differentiated in every generation, as life flows onward. Or, in other language, the experience of one generation imparted to a succeeding one, awakens in consciousness and reason, broader and clearer ideas upon similar subjects, or perhaps brings to light new and heretofore unknown subjects. Yet even this would produce but slight results without organization. Consequently, there must be elements of human progress which have not yet been referred to, and which can only be ascertained by an analytical and synthetical investigation of the history which has been enacted and recorded in its development.

Commencing with the history of Greece, we find the earliest known inhabitants were the Pelasgi, an agricultural people dwelling in walled towns. Aside from a few fragments of massive stone masonry, terra-cotta urns and other utensils, nothing is definitely known of the arts or literature of this people worthy of notice in this brief history.

Veritable Greek history commences with the conquest of the Pelasgi by a colony from Asia. Of this conquering race, the present received opinion is that it separated from the progenitors of the Medo-Persians in the regions of the Persian Gulf, in company with the ancestors of the Romans; that during their migration they acquired a small degree of civilization, and, finally separating, one portion passing into Italy, the other into Greece, conquered and amalgamated with the Pelasgi, thus forming what was known as the Hellenic race, consisting of many tribes, yet having a common language and common religion. Now, this amalgamation of races in different conditions of civilization, and from different climes, must have given a new impetus to sensuous emotion, and thus produced new and varied images to the imagination; and hence we perceive a translucent background to mythical history.

This much is literally true: civilization commenced by the founding of cities and towns, and the organization of systematic labor in the form of agriculture, mechanic arts, and commerce. Yet this did not necessitate the building of temples, the carving of images, or the offering of sacrifices in gratitude or propitiation. Consequently, there must have been, as there still is, other impulses and emotions which elevate man above the mere tilling of the soil for food, or erecting habitations to protect them from the elements.

It may be true that neither Jupiter, Minerva, or any of the so-called heathen gods, were veritable deity; yet the adoration which the Greeks paid to them was a fact, prompted doubtless by that innate sentiment of man which prompts him to attribute all phenomena to Deity, or a First Cause.

The statues they wrought and the temples they erected, to commemorate the acts and attributes of some special deity, became living objects of beauty. They also became a record of man's ideal conceptions and emotions in a certain condition of civilization, and under the influence of certain religious ideas.

No one now believes Jupiter or Minerva to be veritable deity, yet no one will presume to assert that Greek art did not then, as it still does, contain true principles of beauty of form and harmony of proportions. Thus much of truth, at least, did the Greeks develop while under the influence of their infantile conception of an anthropomorphite polytheism.

It does appear, however, that the principles of art which the Greeks developed, were not so much the specialties of Greek idiosyncrasies or Greek institutions, as they were the generic principles which emanate from the rhythm of man's physical, moral, and mental organization, since those laws still form the basis of design in all compositions of constructive art.

The earliest mental impressions of the child are the nursery songs, then the amusing or marvelous stories, and finally the romance songs of the hero and the lover. But the nursery songs of a nation commenced at the point where childhood verges into manhood—at the heroic.

The Greeks had three forms of poetry, the epic, the lyric, and the tragic. The two former will be described as immediately related to the development of art. The earliest form was the epic, which treated of the martial deeds of heroes. It was recited upon battle-fields, in camps, and upon festal days, to inspire the courage of the soldiers, the enthusiasm of the patriot, and in honor of a heroic ancestry.

The subjects of these poems were represented as having once been the rulers of tribes and nations, and as the founders of cities and states. Epic poetry, therefore, was the dawning light of civilization, just rising, as it were, above the horizon of ignorance and barbarism. Its heroes were apotheosized, and the adoration paid them became the national form of religion.

If we take from Greek history its legends and its heroes, upon what does its epic poetry rest? From what source would spring spontaneous emotion?—where the grand central figure, the attractive magnet, around which all individualities center, to organize and initiate a national civilization.

It is true, Greek legendary history appears improbable, even absurd; yet history was born in the lap of ignorance and credulity, before reason was developed upon a thesis of rational observation.

Yet, as that sort of knowledge was not essential to sensuous emotion or imaginary creations, consequently, poetry and art were the primary mediums for the dissemination and perpetuation of ideas.

That which was subjective imagery, became an objective reality by an evolution of the will, prompted by faith and desire. The ideals may not have been absolute verities, yet they none the less expressed the sentiments and belief of the age, and thus became the subjects of legends, which are essential to the development of poetry and art.

Hence, the elements essential to man's development are latent in his nature, and hence the awakening of poetic sentiment and art imagery are the dawning lights of civilization.

Man cannot pass beyond himself in sympathies or passions, and hence all his ideal creations are but the exaggeration, expansion, and elevation of those sentiments and passions of which he himself is the type. Consequently, the transition from a savage to a civilized condition, is the development of poetry, art, literature, science, agriculture, and mechanics, through the joint action of sensuous emotion and non-sensuous reason. It is the homogeneity of thought, and delicacy of body, which causes the sensibility of youth; and, consequently, every incident which affects the mind, produces either pleasure or pain; thus leaving an indelible impress upon the tablet of the mind. We may attribute the never-fading beauty of Greek art to the fact that it was the embodiment of the poetic imagery of a youthful people, whose imagination was not influenced by precedent, nor did it spring from the theologic idea of an offended and revengeful deity. They believed the gods dwelt near them, had the immediate control of human affairs, and that men were the children of the gods.

The Greek school of constructive art, unlike all others, had its origin almost in the infancy of the nation. This has its explanation in the fact, that it was fanciful in its use, as well as ideal in its decoration. The Greek temple was not a structure for utility in the same sense as a cathedral, a town-hall, or a state-house ; it was almost as purely ideal in its use, as in its ornamentation. Consequently, it did not require a national growth to call it into existence, as has been the case with all subsequent schools. And yet the temple had its use in Greek civilization, since it became the grand central figure in the composition of their social economy.

Lyric poetry followed the epic. The hero had

gone to his long home; he had won battles, conquered countries, founded cities and governments, decreed laws for their government; his descendants wept over his grave, celebrated his apotheosis, wrought statues in imitation of his person, and reared temples to commemorate his heroic and virtuous deeds.

In the lyric we have the sympathetic and the pathetic, the expression of the poet's own sentiments and emotions, in place of the description of the person and acts of another, as in the epic.

Lyric poetry sounds like the expression of the reconciliation of two once contending, but now reconciled and united races. The union had warmed and enlivened the blood, enlivened the emotions, and expanded the ideal imagery of the mind, yet left a vague but indelible impression upon the memory of the strifes and contentions of the past. Consequently, poetry became the *alma mater* of art. The desire to give visible expression to the attributes of their hero-gods, as described by the poets, developed sculpture; and the desire to perpetuate the memory of their heroic acts, developed temple building, or the art of decorative construction. Consequently, the origin and development of plastic and constructive art was nearly simultaneous in Greece.

The earliest specimens of both were very rude as compared with their later works; and yet, from inception to culmination, the same leading ideas are apparent. The primitive symbols of their gods were rough blocks of stone; and to invest them with a sacred character, it was claimed they had descended from the clouds. Upon these rough blocks, the sculptor made his first effort to develop the human form, first by a rude outline of the head, then the shoulders, arms, and other portions, and gradually the human form was developed in marble; and the art of sculpture was inaugurated.

The earliest Greek temples were massive, plain, and ill proportioned, as compared with their later works. Yet, upon close inspection, the difference appears more in the mode of treatment than in the subject-matter treated upon. In the description of the temples in detail, it will appear that the same primary ideas are present, from their first inception to their culmination.

Every Greek temple was a complete whole within itself; you could neither add to, nor take from, without destroying the symmetry of the whole structure.

The chief objects of all Greek temples were the same, namely, for external effect, more than for internal use. Consequently, their architects were in no way conditioned in their designs by the requirements of utility. Now, this limit of the object was the immediate cause of the development of forms and proportions to such comparative perfection.

The art of adapting structures to any and all purposes, was not developed in the Greek school; consequently, the science of construction was but partially developed. Yet ornamentation was developed to the highest degree it has yet attained.

The success of the Greeks in architecture may be attributed to two causes: first, to their adhering substantially to a single model; second, in their emulation to perfect it, they reduced their ideal standard of harmony and proportion to a comparatively perfect system. Whatever the Greeks may have borrowed from foreign sources, it had very little influence upon the final development of their school of constructive art.

To admit that the Egyptians had used the post and lintel system of construction prior to the Greeks, is to admit that they had discovered one of the two modes of construction known to the building art, which are, namely, the post and lintel, or stone type; and the pier and arch, or brick type. Of these two modes, the Greeks used only the former; and by making the lower diameter of the column the standard of measurement, by dividing its diameter into sixty parts, called minutes, thus gave proportions to every member of the structure, and thus even determined the width, length, and height of the structure itself.

A careful examination of the proportions of Greek temples will show that the solids and voids bear nearly the same relative proportion to each other in their earlier as well as later works, whether the columns are 4½ or 6 diameters high.

Hence, it is rational to infer that they had, from the commencement, an ideal law of proportion; and by adhering to it through a series of structures, finally reduced it to a science, which continues to be the law of proportion for constructive art at the present time; for the simple reason, no subsequent school has developed laws superior, or even equal in perfection.

Had there been a greater variety of purposes to subserve, or greater subordination to special uses, there would have been less positivity in their laws of proportion, and less harmony in the forms and outline of decoration. Having but the one grand object in view—to achieve the grand and beautiful—the subject and object were conditioned only by the limits of the genius of the artist.

Having adhered to unity of design, they attained to comparative perfection of outline, and harmony of proportions, by experimenting upon a series of structures.

The most ancient monument of Greek art known to us, is the ruins of the temple of Corinth; but whether it originally had a cell, roof, and pediments, or simply columns supporting an entablature, is likely to remain a mystery.

But the next in chronologic order—the temple of Ægina—was a very perfect specimen of a Doric hexastyle temple. The truth is, nearly all the ancient monuments of Greece, of which anything definite is known, were executed during the period 479 B. C. to 420 B. C., during the political and intellectual ascendency of Athens. Of these structures, the oldest is supposed to be the temple of Theseus, a Doric hexastyle, with columns a little more than 5½ diameters high, well proportioned entablature, with sculptured frieze, and alto figures in the tympanum representing the exploits of the hero to whom the temple was dedicated.

It is claimed by some authors that the temple of Theseus furnished the model for the Parthenon. Be that as it may, the Parthenon was constructed about thirty years later than the Theseum, and was another of the series of temple structures—each successive structure seeking to excel its predecessor.

The Greeks practiced the same principles of composition in all their temples. As an example, a hexastyle temple had always thirteen columns upon the flanks, and an octastyle seventeen. The proportions of the entablatures to the diameter of the columns were nearly the same, whether they were four or six diameters high, thus indicating that all parts of the structure derived their proportions from the diameter of the columns. This law of proportion was also applied to the solids and the voids, as the five intercolumniations of a hexastyle temple were nearly equal in superficial area to the six columns and their superincumbent mass. The vertical lines of the columns were slightly curved, and the angle columns were slightly increased in size to balance the effect of the greater space upon the outer side.

Greek genius exhausted itself in combining beauty of form with harmony of proportion ; and in so doing it achieved greater perfection than has since been attained in that special direction. The secret of its success is, that it subordinated utility to the development of beauty. Whatever use may have been made of the interior of their temples, it was at all times subordinated to external effect.

Nor do we find different modes of construction or of composition in the application of the different orders. In the use of either, the same objects are sought, the difference consisting merely in the modes of ornamentation. The Doric and Ionic were the only orders used by the Greeks in temple building; and as they were both the products of the same race, aiming to achieve the same grand objects, consequently, they did not vary materially in plan or mode of construction. The Doric may be said to express the masculine, the Ionic the feminine. The former is drawn with a bold and masculine hand, the latter with more grace and delicacy of expression. It is claimed by some authors,—Mr. Fergusson in particular,—that many of the ornaments used in the Ionic order were borrowed from Persian art. Now, it is not material to our subject whether they did or did not borrow certain modes of construction, and certain forms of ornament, since it must be conceded the Greeks did embody pagan esthetics in a systematic school of art; and to do that, forms must be used; and whether they were original with them, or had previously been used by others, does not materially affect the question of the originality of Greek art. The genius was not so much in the mere origination of forms, as in their combination and relative proportions of quantities, which enabled them to express certain ideas, qualities, and attributes. This alphabet of allegory, it must be admitted, the Greeks systematized and arranged; and yet it appears to have been more the genius of humanity than the mere idiosyncrasy of the Greeks, since other nations have used the same, or a similar language, to express similar emotions.

The fact that Greek art continues to be the admiration of the civilized world, is the most convincing proof that it was the offspring of human emotion and aspiration. The unity and simplicity of plan and construction of Greek temples, which in the nature of its composition gave beauty of form the precedence of utility, accounts for the fact that the uneducated have a higher appreciation of Greek art than those who have a greater knowledge of the true meaning and objects of art at the present day.

The individuality of character of a Greek temple gives it a completeness within itself, which no other class of structures ever possessed ; and this is the great secret of their universal admiration. Like the human body, they could not be enlarged, changed, or modified, without destroying their beauty.

It is generally conceded that the development of sculpture preceded that of architecture ; and as many of their artists practiced both arts, it is rational to suppose they were indebted to their knowledge of the anatomy of the human body for their ideas of the laws of proportion in architecture.

Both sculpture and architecture emanated from the same grand ideal conception, namely, to embody in imperishable forms the attributes and acts of their hero-gods. Now, when we perceive that their hero-gods were but an idealized type of themselves, we also perceive the Greek created his gods and his arts from his own potentiality—and hence another secret of their perpetual beauty.

It is generally believed that Euclid was the inventor or discoverer of the principles of geometry, as he was the earliest writer upon that subject; yet it is a singular fact that, years before his time, the Greeks had used nearly every form known in geometry in the construction of their temples. Even their moldings were eccentric curves, similar to those described by conic sections; although it is claimed conic sections were first discovered in the school of Plato, some years after the completion of the Parthenon.

From these facts it may be inferred that geometry and mathematics are adjuncts of the genius of construction, and are ever present to lend their aid, as the development of the art may require.

Art, literature, and philosophy were developed nearly simultaneously; and yet it does not appear that philosophy exercised any special influence outside the schools where it was taught. Art was almost exclusively devoted to religion, while philosophy was announcing principles directly in conflict with the state religion. Yet philosophy did not put forth any broad or matured system of political economy.

While they had a common language, a common religion, a common school of art and literature, yet they never united as a nation under one government. No form of government ever adopted by a civilized people has proved more ephemeral than those established by the Greeks. Turn from the study of their poetry, arts, literature, and philosophy, to the study of their political economy, and mark the contrast. Great as they were as scholars, artists, and captains,—and this applies to individuals more than to the mass of the nation,—yet they did not attain to a political status essential to a national unity. The governments they did establish, alternated between the worst forms of despotism and the broadest forms of democracy. It is true, however, those states were the most prosperous, and attained to the highest degree of civilization, that adopted liberal forms of government. Yet they were intolerant toward all other governments, sought to extend their jurisdiction by conquest and by establishing colonies for the commercial benefit of the parent country only. Perhaps the geographical formation of the country was such as naturally to induce a partition of the inhabitants into small communities.

This was the condition of the Pelasgi at the time of the Hellenic conquest; and that event does not appear to have materially contributed toward a national unity, although it gave an impetus to the development of the primary elements of civilization.

Nothing is more essential to a people rising out of barbarism toward a civilized state, than expansion; but, unfortunately for the Grecian states, they could not expand—with few exceptions—that is, they could neither enlarge their geographical boundaries nor disseminate their political principles without destroying each other. No one state became sufficiently influential or powerful to control all others, and hence Greece became an easy conquest to a powerful external enemy.

Greek civilization was developed upon the ideal of a symbolized religion with a plurality of gods, to no one of which was attributed powers and attributes superior to all others. This had its influence upon their political as well as religious institutions; thus far at least, that every city, tribe, and nation had its own special deity, who was supposed to assume the special guardianship of their temporal affairs. This created an emulation among the different states and cities in arts and arms, which had a tendency to separate, rather than to unite them in a common nationality.

While the climate of Greece and the aspects of nature may have been favorable to develop an active imagination, and to suggest images of beauty, yet the same influences may not have suggested to the mind the advantages of a united political nationality.

It was this individuality of character of their political and religious institutions, which stamped upon their temple architecture such marked individuality of character, and identified it with no distinct subject save that which related to the person and acts of the hero-god it was erected to commemorate.

It is to be remembered, however, the Greeks had not the benefit of the political experience of other nations to aid them in the organizations of their own institutions, and hence were comparatively ignorant upon that subject, however enlightened they may have been upon other subjects.

The science of government is more than a mere invention; it is the product of experience and mental development; the resultant of social organizations; and, consequently, developed in various ways and in various degrees; while religion, the *alma mater* of art, is purely the property of the individual; and hence, art is spontaneous, and in its resources independent of experience. It must be admitted, however, that the arts of one generation or age have an influence upon those which follow; yet not perhaps so much from mere imitation, as from suggestion, that modification and development are achieved, in accordance with the requirements of the modifications of social organizations.

It has before been stated, an active religious faith was the origin of Greek art; and hence it may be assumed that any purely original system of religion will develop an original school of art in harmony with its own ideal spirit.

It is epually true, a nation or people that grow fro infancy to power and empire, if they adopt a system of religion already developed, they will also adopt the system of ornamentation which it has developed ; modifying construction to meet the necessities of their own organizations. No system of religion, however, has ever produced more than one original school of art; while it may have subserved the purposes of various forms of government.

What caused the peculiar development of Greek civilization in that special locality, and in that particular era, is a mooted question, and one that is not likely soon to be answered to the satisfaction of an inquiring mind. Nevertheless, there must have been a cause, but whether hidden beyond the research of man, is yet to be determined. What may be here said upon the subject, is to be taken for nothing more than what appears to the author as rational conjecture, based upon certain well authenticated historical facts.

The romantic and brilliant character of Grecian fable could have been the product of none other than a vivid poetic imagination, which, doubtless, was the immediate cause of the rise and development of poetry and art. But the grand question is, What caused the Greeks to be more imaginative, poetic, and vivacious, than the cognate races of adjoining countries? To which inquiry may be replied, that one of the probable causes was the peculiar aspects of the country, the climate, and soil. Greece is perhaps the most mountainous country in Europe; its surface is divided into a number of small plains entirely surrounded by mountains, or open merely to the sea. At the time of the birth of Greek civilization, these ranges of mountains must have been covered with variegated foliage, extending up the sides in various heights, and the lofty peaks were covered with snow, while the plains beneath were covered with a flowering foliage, which must have produced scenery unsurpassed by any upon the globe. Its climate was mild, with an atmosphere clear and brilliant.

The inhabitants of all Alpine countries are more romantic and poetic in feeling and sentiment than are those who dwell upon the level plains; for the simple reason, mountainous scenery impresses itself more indelibly upon the senses, and thus awakens à more vivid imagination, and a higher poetic sentiment. That this alone will lead to the highest degree of civilization, is not claimed; but that it is the first awakening to a progressive civilization, there is convincing historic evidence.

But the most rational cause of the impetus given to the development of early Greek civilization, was the conquest and amalgamation of two races of dissimilar mental development. As to who the conquering race really were—whether Asiatic or a superior tribe of the Pelasgi—does not materially affect our subject. That they were more civilized than the local habitants, there is no doubt; but the more important fact is, that the character of conqueror and conquered were soon lost in the fusion of the general mass.

This fusion of the blood of two distinct races or tribes in different conditions of development, quickened mental impulse, enlivened and vivified sensuous emotion, created new images in the world of imagination, which fancied it saw the heroes of the conquest raised to the dignity of gods.

Whether the siege of Troy was a myth, and the Homeric poems a collection of epics composed at various eras, is not so important to our subject as is the fact that epic poetry was the earliest indication of an awakening civilization. The legends of the exploits of heroes described by those epics stimulated the desire to personate them in statuary; and to delineate their heroic acts, they invented ornamental construction, or temple building, upon the exterior of which they sculptured symbolic forms and images, expressing certain heroic acts.

Now, the radical differences between the Greek and Egyptian schools were, that the former was demonstrative of ideas, acts, persons, attributes; while the latter was merely suggestive of ideas and essence, but incapable of demonstration by personal acts or attributes; and, hence, development was a mere repetition of the same forms; its indefinite character was the cause of its failure to organize and develop a distinct system of ornamentation.

On the other hand, the individuality of character, definite attributes, and distinctive acts which the Greeks attributed to their gods, gave distinctness and variety to symbolic forms, which were capable of a great variety of expression, by varied combinations of forms, and varied amounts of substance.

The Greek school was a perfect success, from the fact that every form, ornament, or symbol, had a distinct and significant meaning; and nothing was piled or spread on for the sake of mere ornament.

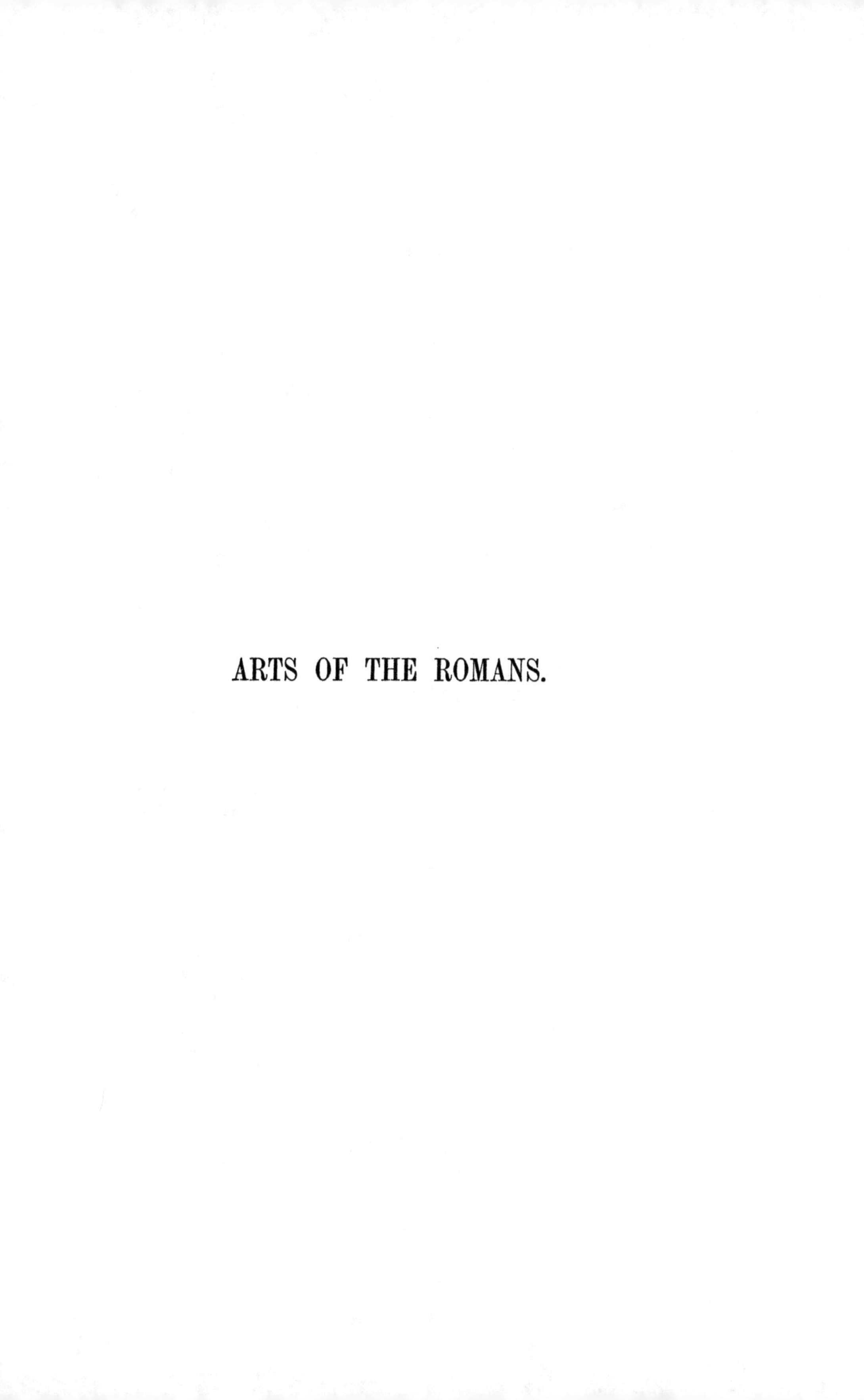

ARTS OF THE ROMANS.

ARTS OF THE ROMANS.

The early history of the Romans contains very little that is legendary, poetic, imaginative, or heroic.

The legend of Romulus and Remus appears to have been an invention of priests of a later period, to invest the history of the origin of the Roman people with somewhat of a sacred character. But it was too material in spirit to inspire a lyric, or awaken an imaginative or artistic spirit.

Nor was the legend of the forcible abduction of the Sabine women of a nature to awaken a spirit of poetry or art. History gives a very different account of the manner of the entry of the Sabines into Rome. The earliest authentic history indicates that the palatine was seized and fortified by a band of wandering outlaws, who had organized under competent leaders for the purpose of subsisting upon the plunder of the adjoining country,

As the Sabine territories were the nearest of access, they became the theater of their first depredations; and as the Sabines were a warlike people, the conflicts became severe and protracted, and finally terminated in the settlement of a Sabine colony within the walls of the palatine. This original seat of the Romans was situated in the angle of the territories of three considerable tribes or nations: the Sabines, the Latins, and the Etruscans; all of which eventually became amalgamated with, and composed a portion of the Roman people.

The question, therefore, is, What were the peculiar mental, moral, and physical qualities of these several nations, which, when amalgamated, composed the peculiar idiosyncrasies of the early Romans?

From the Sabines they inherited their most prominent national characteristic—military genius. From the Latins they derived their language, their knowledge of husbandry, and their primitive simplicity of tastes and manners. From the Etruscans they derived their first elements of art,—but especially that element which pertains more directly to construction than to ornamentation. From what source they derived their system of religion, is not very clear; the subject with them was a secondary one, as compared with the material interests of the state.

History is not clear as to the progress of, and definite time of conquest of the early Romans; nor is this work intended as a literal history of the military or civil transactions of any particular nation; but such historical facts are cited, as most forcibly illustrate the development of peculiar idiosyncrasies, and in their manifestations discover the cause, and the necessity, of the peculiar development of their arts.

The earliest form of Roman government appears to have been a species of oligarchy, with an elective monarchy as its chief executive. This form of government existed 244 years, and is said to have included the reigns of seven monarchs.

This was the mythical age of Roman history, yet we fail to discover the presence of a poetic spirit, or the manifestation of those idealized, mental elements which were so conspicuous in the mythical age of Greek history, and which made them poets, artists, religious enthusiasts, and eventually philosophers. There was nothing of the epic or the lyric spirit in the legends of Roman history. The legend of Romulus and Remus was neither poetic, suggestive, nor aspiring; neither was the story of the forcible abduction of the Sabine women a lofty conception of the heroic.

Therefore, the origin of Roman art must be sought in material necessities, more than in idealized mental aspirations. It is not to be presumed, however, that the Romans were without ideal sentiment; but it was of that peculiar nature which gravitated toward the material more than to the ideal; which made them soldiers, statesmen, and engineers, more than religious enthusiasts, poets, artists, or philosophers.

The first impetus given to Roman art, was their contact with the Etruscans; and the tradition that the later kings were of Etruscan origin, may, or may not, be true; yet there is little doubt, the superior civilization of the Etruscans, as compared with other cognate nations, gave them a superior influence at court, which made them the leading artists and scholars, as well as statesmen.

Etruscan art, however, had not the elements of expansion or development which were susceptible of reduction to a system by a series of experiments. As the Romans learned construction only of the Etruscans, and as they had not the genius to invent a system of ornamentation, their decorative school was developed by the aid of Greek genius.

But as the larger class of Roman edifices were for secular purposes, from necessity they secularized and utilized Greek ideal art, without destroying its forms of beauty; and from necessity, they simultaneously developed the pier and arch mode of construction. In accomplishing this, they also effected a transition of purpose, from structures for external effect, to structures for internal use.

Now, while the Roman school was not original in its system of ornamentation, yet it was original in its construction and adaptation to purpose; and as a study, is, perhaps, the most instructive school yet developed. Yet, in the analysis of their early works, we discover the useful more than the ornamental—a reflective more than an imaginative spirit.

That spirit of emulation in arts, literature, and philosophy, which animated the Greeks, does not appear in Roman history. To them, it appears, conquest and dominion were the only subjects and objects worthy the attention of a great nation.

Although it may at present be difficult to define the practical difference of Greek and Roman genius, yet it is clear they both formed a part of the same great social system—which originated with the Greeks, and culminated in the Roman empire. While nearly all Greek monuments of art were ideal—for external effect—yet by far the larger portion of Roman works were constructed for internal use; and yet the two schools were similar in their ornamentation.

The Romans learned of the Etruscans the use of the arch, and made very general use of it in construction, which finally became a principal feature in their school of ornamentation. They also made use of the circle for the plan of temples and other structures, which they also borrowed from the Etruscans, but their origin was Pelasgic.

The Roman school was heterogeneous in its origin, which was a counterpart of the heterogeneous nature of the Roman people; and the absence of any artistic development during the early life of the nation, may be attributed to their austerity of manners and domestic feuds.

Upon the expulsion of their kings, followed a great moral warfare between the patricians and plebeians, as to political privileges, and what should be the social status of the latter.

It was through the intrigues of the patricians with the plebeians that royalty was overthrown; but when it was accomplished, the patricians were in no haste to fulfill their promises to the plebeians. Finding themselves deceived, and likely to become the mere servants of the patricians, they chose their own leaders, and retired from the city. Whereupon, being hard pressed by their enemies, the patricians were compelled to make certain concessions, and the people returned to the city.

Having gained this first point, they did not cease in their demands, nor relax their energies, until all political and social distinctions were abolished. From that time forward, Rome was a republic in spirit as well as in name, until military success elevated her rulers to a daring and unscrupulous ambition, and the acquisition of great wealth corrupted her people, and the republic was crushed out under the weight of military despotism. Yet, notwithstanding their uniform success in war, it was nearly five centuries after the founding of Rome before they were the complete masters of Italy. One of their last conquests in Italy was the Greek city of Tarentum, which they plundered of its precious works of art, and carried them in triumph to Rome. These were the first works of ornament and luxury known to have been introduced into the capital of republican simplicity and military heroism. During the next century after the conquest of Italy, Rome made herself master of the islands in the Mediterranean, large territories in Spain and Africa, and nearly the whole of Greece.

It was during this period that her great increase in wealth, and consequent social transition, created the necessity for a great variety of structures.

The people inhabiting the shores of the Mediterranean, which had become subject to Roman rule, possessed great wealth; and the cities of Greece, especially, possessed large collections of precious works of art, many of which, through various means, found their way to the city of Rome. As the capital of the empire, it became the centre of commerce, and thus gave rise to the necessity of those structures termed Basilicas. The custom of celebrating their victories by a grand procession, displaying their prisoners and booty, originated the custom of erecting triumphal arches to perpetuate their memory.

As the city increased in population, a supply of fresh water became indispensable for health, and thus gave rise to the necessity for constructing those artificial water-courses, termed aqueducts.

An increase of wealth and power gave a license to luxury, the chief of which was the indulgence in the bath; thus creating the necessity for those structures termed public baths.

The passion for public amusements, and the idle habits of the people, especially during the later years of the republic as well as the empire, created the necessity for those colossal structures termed amphitheaters.

Now, in all the above enumerated structures, there appears a tendency toward the material more than to the ideal; there was nothing in the life or temperament of the Romans which indicated a genius for creating images of beauty. It may be said of them, they were great mechanics, but not great artists; they developed a system of construction, but not of ornamentation. Unlike the Greeks, the drama of their life is written in prose, not in poetry; religion was an institution necessary to the welfare of the state, more than the zeal and enthusiasm of the individual.

It is true, they constructed temples, some of which were fashioned after their own models; yet all were Greek in style of ornamentation. But by far the larger portion of their ornamental structures were for secular purposes. Now, in every stage of the development of Roman art, it tends to utility; yet, it is clear, the Romans made greater progress in the development of social economy, and, hence, greater progress toward a high state of civilization, than did the Greeks. In this, the Romans developed the art of civilizing a nation, while the Greeks developed the art of civilizing the individual. Both adhered substantially to the same system of religion, both adopted similar forms of government, consequently, must have had similar arts and literature. The secular school of the Romans was essential to give pagan art its full development, which it never would have attained under the patronage of Greek social economy. As it was susceptible of variety in combination of forms, it was also capable of variety in application of purpose.

There is nearly the same elasticity in constructive art, that there is in language; the peculiar forms which constructive art developed to express certain ideas, are susceptible of new combinations and arrangements, for the purpose of expressing new ideas, nearly to the same extent as are the letters of the alphabet. Constructive art has two primary elements, namely, external effect, and internal use, neither one of which, considered abstractly, embraces the whole of the subject. It is therefore clear that the highest order of constructive art is that which most perfectly serves the purposes of utility, with a constructive decoration that shall clearly, and pleasingly, express the purposes intended to subserve in the internal distribution. The Romans, adhering to these principles—with a system of ornamentation already developed—created a school of greater significance than that of the Greeks, from the fact of its greater variety of adaptation to purpose, and consequent greater variety in construction and ornamentation. To make this last proposition more clear, it is essential to investigate, with some minuteness, Roman edifices in connection with the history of their origin, and the cause and necessities which produced their construction.

In the city of Rome, there is but one temple structure remaining which furnishes a clear idea of its primitive character, and that is the structure known as the Pantheon. The cell or body of the temple is circular, constructed of bricks, and hence is more Etruscan than Greek; while its octastyle Corinthian portico is Greco-Roman in design. Now, whether this temple was originally constructed with or without the portico, is not very essential; in either case it is a very clear exposition of the eclecticism of Roman art. Their parallelogram temples were not uniformly designed upon the rigid principles as were the Greek temples. As an instance, their tetrastyle temples had not always nine columns upon their flanks, nor their hexastyle thirteen, nor their octastyle seventeen, as had all Greek temples of a corresponding size. Neither did they observe the Greek rules in the distribution of their intercolumniations.

The omission of the last mentioned rules gave great expansiveness to construction, as well as elasticity to ornamentation; yet it was at the sacrifice of purity of the principles of columnar art. This was, however, a necessity with the Romans, since their social and political institutions were much more expansive, and founded upon a broader basis than were those of the Greeks; and although they had not the genius to create the poetic imagery of art, yet they had the talents to build up a great empire, and had thus created the necessity for a great variety of ornamental structures.

Therefore, it is not to the Roman school that we look for ideal forms of beauty, but rather for the principles of construction and modes of adaptation. Since it was not possible for the Romans to apply Greek or Etruscan structures to all their public and private wants, they had the ingenuity to retain the spirit of their ornamentation, and apply it to structures suited to their own peculiar wants and necessities. This they accomplished by retaining the proportions of the columns, the principal features and proportions of the entablature, but varied the intercolumniations, as the necessity of the case required.

The Romans had five orders of architecture, namely, the Tuscan, the Doric, the Ionic, the Corinthian, and the Composite. Their Tuscan order was but a plainer form of the Greek Doric; while their Composite was, what its name imports, a compound of the Greek Ionic and Corinthian orders.

They modified the severity of the Greek Doric, by adding a molded base, diminished the size of the shaft, increased the members of the capital, retained the essential features of the entablature, but varied the distance between columns. They also modified the Greek Ionic order, but not for the better, nor did they make very frequent use of it.

The Corinthian was their favorite order, and the only Greek order they improved upon, for large structures. It must be admitted, the Roman Corinthian was superior to the Greek. It was the counterpart of Roman mind, its elements were expansive, flowery, grandiloquent, was susceptible of great extremes, and its application was almost universal in their temple structures. Many of their structures were of the circular form, which produced variety in effect, and also a heterogeneous character to the principles of construction. The tendency of Roman art was to secular, more than to sacred uses; and to gradually emancipate itself from those rigid laws of harmony and proportion which were established in the development of Greek art. As the Greeks rigidly adhered to the post and lintel system of construction, to secularize their school of ornamentation was to adapt it to the pier and arch system of construction.

This was accomplished by increasing the spaces between columns, diminishing the size of the entablature, until the increased space and slender entablature required an arch between columns for its support; and, finally, placing the colonnade against the face of a wall, thus transforming the colonnade into an arcade.

Among the earliest structures in the pier and arch style, were gateways at the terminus of roads and bridges. Before the conquest of Greece, these structures were simple, plain masonry; but in the later years of the republic, they were made the symbols of victory, and thus became objects of personal and national vanity; and in decorating them, they violated the established laws of composition, and exhausted their ingenuity in straining after novel and striking effects.

But the most extraordinary of structures which originated with the Romans, were their amphitheaters; and the custom which created the necessity for their construction is worthy of notice. It was a very ancient heathen custom to celebrate the funeral rites of heroes slain in battle, with gladiatorial combats. This custom was revived in Rome in the year B. C. 264, when Marcus and Decimus Brutus celebrated the funeral rites of their father. At the termination of the Samnite war, there were gladiatorial exhibitions in honor of those victories; and from that time forward, they were common at nearly all public exhibitions.

In the year B. C. 252, Lucius Metellus celebrated his victories over the Carthagenians by the introduction of elephants into the arena, thus making combats of wild beasts a portion of the entertainment, which eventually led to combats of gladiators and condemned criminals with wild beasts. We have some slight conception of the extent of these brutal and demoralizing exhibitions, when we are informed that Titus gave an exhibition that lasted one hundred days, and that Trajan celebrated his victory over Decebalus by the exhibition of ten thousand gladiators. These exhibitions were originally given in the open air; but as they became more frequent and extensive, temporary wood structures were used, which underwent various modifications, from part wood and part stone, to structures entirely of stone. So passionately attached to these brutal exhibitions did the Roman people become, that they became a part of the police regulations, and the government erected permanent structures for their special accommodation in all towns where there was a permanent military station.

These buildings were all nearly upon the same plan, but varying in size and decoration. The largest of these structures known, is the one at Rome, known as the Coliseum, which is elliptical in form; the largest diameter 615 feet, and the lesser 510 feet. The exterior was decorated with four orders of architecture. The first, or lower order, was Doric, the second Ionic, the third Corinthian, and the fourth Composite. In the spaces between the columns of the three lower orders were large open arches; while the fourth had a continuous wall, for the purpose, as is generally supposed, of holding the apparatus for spreading a canvas roof over the vast arena, which had capacity for seating eighty thousand persons.

In constructive science, this building has few rivals; and its vast size gives it a solemn grandeur which overshadows its artistic defects.

It was in the construction of the above described buildings, that orders above orders were first used on the exterior, as ornamentation. They had been so used for construction in interiors before.

The custom of bathing was one of the chief sources of luxury in excess, practiced by the Romans.

The custom was no doubt borrowed from the east; but in its incipient stage, like most customs, was for sanitary purposes. Marcus Agrippa, while discharging the duties of Ædile, erected, in the year B. C. 33, one hundred and sixty places where the people could be accommodated with free baths. Following this popular measure, most of the emperors who courted favor with the people, erected public baths, the most extensive and magnificent of which were those of Nero, Titus, Caracalla, and Diocletian. Baths were also attached to the residences of wealthy citizens, but were used only on special occasions, as it was the custom for all classes to visit the public baths.

Hot, cold, and vapor baths, with perfuming and anointing, were all indulged in at a single bathing. To such an excess was the habit carried, that Hadrian issued an edict that all public baths should be opened and closed at certain hours of the day. Embraced in the same buildings with the baths, were libraries, corridors for exercise, and halls where poets recited their compositions, and philosophers lectured to their students. Externally, these structures had no great artistic merit, nor even pretensions, constructed chiefly with bricks, and hence did not admit of much constructive ornamentation ; but internally they were decorated with marble columns, statues, stucco work, gilding and painting, in great splendor and profusion.

To obtain some idea of the magnitude of these

structures, it is merely necessary to state that the baths of Diocletian were 1150 feet square, and those of Caracalla 1840 feet long, and 1476 feet wide.

But the buildings which most interest modern society, and which, more than any other class, form the connecting link between the old and the new civilizations, are the basilicas, since they were selected for the models of the first Christian churches. In the infancy of Roman institutions, all business of a public nature was transacted in the forum or public square ; but as the city increased in wealth and population, the business of politics and trade gradually separated, and to each were assigned separate forums.

As trade became a more settled and permanent business, to avoid the inconvenience of the open air, and to subject it to police regulations, it was removed to an apartment connected with a magistrate's residence, where he attended in person, to settle any differences that might arise in the course of trade.

When the republic had grown to an empire, and

commerce forsook its itinerant habits, government provided for its better accommodation by erecting those structures termed basilicas. They were remarkable for their constructive, more than their decorative features, since they were for internal use rather than for external effect. In the provincial towns they were usually oblong rooms, with a semicircular apse at the rear end, in which was placed the magistrate's seat, and were roofed with wood, without internal supports. In the city of Rome there were two classes of basilicas; one in the Grecian post and lintel mode of construction, and the other in the Etrusci-Roman pier and arch mode of construction; the former were roofed with wood, and the latter with a groined vaulting. The two kinds of structures did not represent two distinct elements of commerce, but they were simply the development of the two principles of construction which composed Roman constructive art; and it will be shown hereafter, that one class furnished the model for the Greek churches, and the other class for the Latin churches.

Now, in contrasting the basilica with the

Temple, we perceive there has been a complete transition of purpose, from external effect to internal use. Man has descended from the adoration of the gods to the worship of lucre. Yet, notwithstanding all the admiration that has been bestowed upon the Greek temples, the experiment of adapting their forms to modern uses has proved a failure.

The Romans adhered to the spirit of their ornamentation, but modeled the plans of their edifices to meet the wants of their own social necessities. Nor have the models of Roman structures, with one exception, proved more available for modern uses, than have the Greek models.

Of the character of the dwellings of the people, we know little or nothing; as for their splendid palaces, they have contributed nothing to the plans or arrangements of our modern dwelling. They embraced, it is true, splendid state apartments, courts, temples, fountains, promenades; yet their culinary arrangements bore no comparison to our modern conveniences; and their sleeping apartments were little better than a modern prison cell. From the modern stand-point, they bear evi dence of ostentation more than refinement.

There is no evidence in Roman history of the presence of a poetic, lively, and sensitive imagination. Their authentic history commences with the record of the strifes and contentions of castes—of the patricians and plebeians—for the monopoly of the powers of government. In the absence of a written code of laws, the patricians seized the power, and arrogated to themselves the supreme right to govern. This was not conceded by the plebeians; and the consequence was, a perpetual domestic strife, which was carried to such extremes that foreign wars were frequently resorted to, to save the state from a hopeless anarchy.

During these struggles, both parties were convinced of the necessity of a written code of laws, to serve as a check upon party legislation; and in the year of Rome 304, a system was compiled, in part from existing laws, and in part from Greek laws. What immediate effect these laws had upon the prosperity of the state, or upon personal liberty, it is difficult to decide.

The almost continuous wars in which they were engaged, kept the civil authorities in perpetual agitation; and their functions were frequently suspended by the appointment of a dictator, who was irresponsible to either rulers or people; which fact renders it somewhat difficult to comprehend the principles of equity in their system of jurisprudence. From the organization of the government, the political strife was for the possession of power, more than for the supremacy and perpetuation of any distinctly pronounced principles. The striking feature in their domestic system, is the sacredness of an oath; and it was by uniting the civil and sacerdotal office in the same person, that impressed the people with the idea of the sacred character of law.

It was by the pretense of the sacredness of the sacerdotal office, that the patricians for a time evaded the aspirations of the plebeians to the office of consul; as they claimed, it would be a profanation of the office to be vested in a person of plebeian extraction. And yet their history shows no evidences of a religious enthusiasm, and hence the absence of ideal and poetic sentiments, and the tendency to material pursuits.

If we are to judge from the manner they treated their captives and slaves, their want of gratitude toward those who, at the hazard of life and fortune, had saved the state from sudden and unforeseen perils, we are led to the belief that they were an ambitious, tyrannical, and unfeeling people. Their history clearly proves that a thirst for military fame was the ruling passion of the governing class; that victories won might open the road to the governorship of a province; and peculation, fraud, and oppression, to a fortune.

Such was the character of those who composed the aristocracy of the later days of the republic, and of those who crushed out liberty under the weight of military despotism. Yet it was to this class that Rome mainly owed her fame and her greatness, as well as her weakness. Her military heroes built her temples, her basilicas, her aqueducts, her baths, her amphitheaters; and they also corrupted and oppressed her people, violated her laws, oppressed and ruined her provinces, destroyed her civil liberties, and finally drenched her soil with the blood of her own citizens. From the exhibition of such scenes as the conspiracy of Catiline, the butcheries of Sylla, and the civil strifes of Pompey and Cæsar, we are to infer that all the laws, morality, and religion of the republic were powerless to restrain the unbridled ambition of unscrupulous men. Their institutions were but the creations of a military genius; yet while they had the ability to conquer, and, therefore, to destroy, if not to create, they had the good sense to appreciate the genius of those they conquered.

Therefore, in the plenitude of their power, the arts became essential to minister to sensual appetites, if not to gratify a cultivated and refined taste. Even in philosophy they manifested their tastes for the sensual, as they borrowed the grossest forms of the Greek schools of stoicism and epicurianism.

If the Roman school does not exhibit the evidences of a creative genius, on the other hand it teaches many useful lessons in construction and practical application. In the science of construction, it must be conceded, the Romans stand at the head of the pagan school; and the variety of structures is evidence of a more expansive system of social economy, and a more direct application of the intellectual powers to material prosperity.

The arts of the Greeks and Romans may be said to be portions of the same great social and intellectual system; the former created, the latter applied; the one the school of ideal beauty, the other the school of sensual utility.

The emulation of the Greek cities in arts and in national games, refined, rather than expanded, Greek genius; while the thirst for military fame, and desire for wealth, gave the Romans a broad expanse of mind, but left them neither leisure nor inclination for personal accomplishments; and since they devoted their energies to the acquisition of material things, they devoted their leisure to sensual gratification. The poetic and religious spirit of Greek mind, inclined their arts more to the ideal than the practical; and hence its chief objects were to give external expression to the poetic and religious sentiment of society.

And thus art came into existence from the unconscious egoism of man's nature; for the soul can no more rest without external evidence of its own existence, than it could form a rational belief in the existence of a deity without the evidences of created nature. Nor is the egoism of the Romans less manifest than that of the Greeks; since they applied the ideal beauties of Greek art to the purposes of utility. What was the pleasure of the Greek to produce through the action of his poetic imagination, the unimaginative Roman applied to the gratification of sense.

That they delighted in the contemplation of works of art, there is no rational grounds for doubt; but it was more with the feelings of the sensualist, than of the poet or artist. And yet it is not to be denied that art and literature, even debased and degraded as they eventually became, saved the Romans from declining into utter barbarism for many years after pagan faith was literally dead as a state religion. Greek genius kept the elements of civilization together by ministering to the grosser appetites of man; while at the same time it was planting the seeds of a new faith in the hearts of the poor and oppressed, that was to raise out of chaos a new church founded upon a spiritual faith. So interwoven were paganism and licentiousness, that the rich and governing class clung with tenacity to its decaying institutions, long after the regenerating spirit of Christianity had found its way to the hearts of the poor and the ignorant mass of the nation. The decline of pagan institutions was the cause of the decline of classic or pagan art, and it slumbered in obscurity until the rise of Christian institutions awakened human genius to a new sphere of life, faith, and hope.

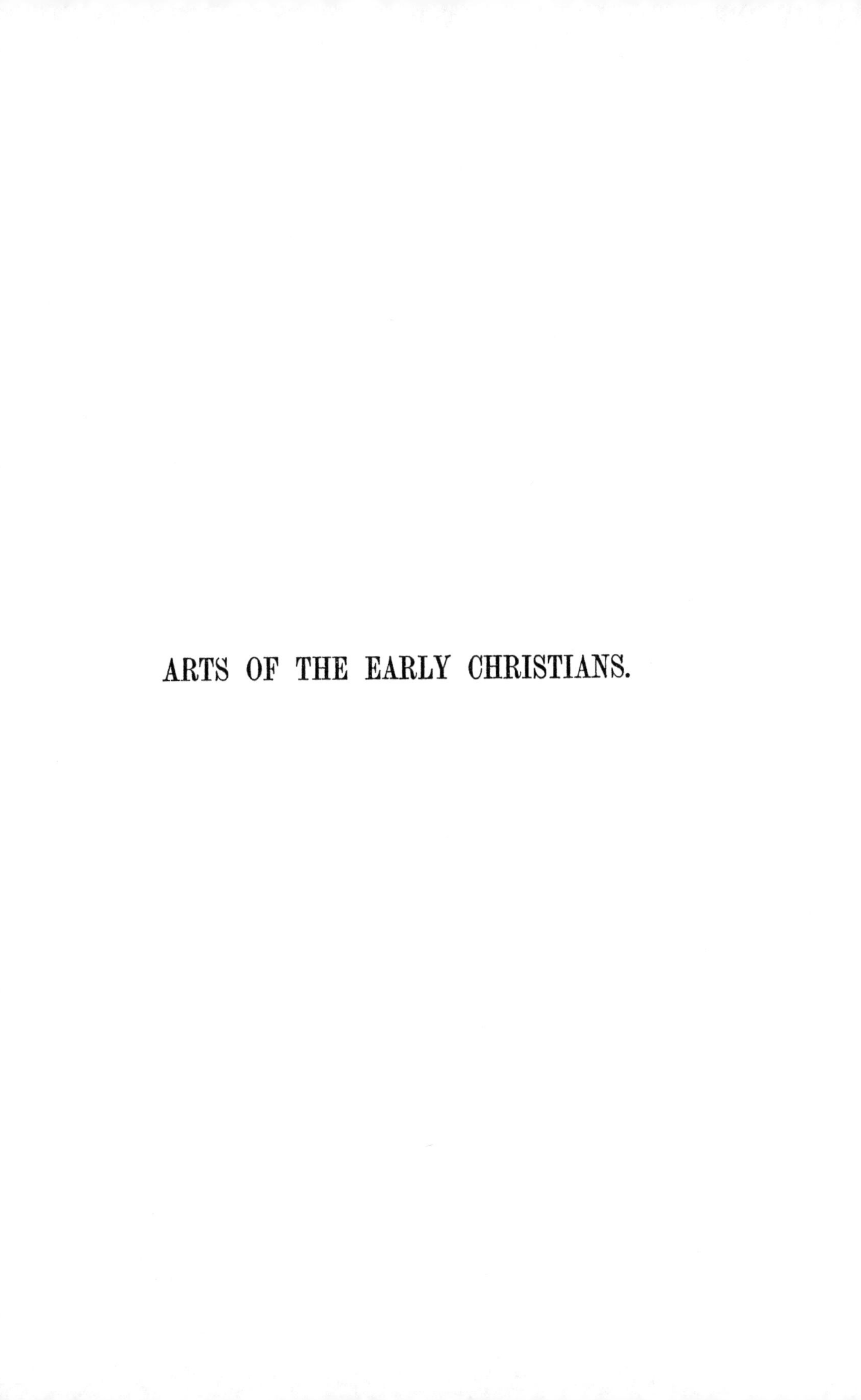

ARTS OF THE EARLY CHRISTIANS.

ARTS OF THE EARLY CHRISTIANS.

It is not perhaps strictly within the province of this work to comment upon the probable or improbable interposition of Divine agency in the affairs of mankind; yet there is one remarkable event in history which cannot well be passed by unnoticed; and that is the peculiar condition of the civilized world at the advent of Christ. Although he was of Jewish origin, and claimed his mission was to teach his Jewish brethren, yet the fruits of his doctrines have chiefly sprung from the Gentiles. This might be accounted for upon philosophic grounds, from the fact that faith in paganism was then declining, and, with perhaps the exception of the Jews, the whole Roman empire was without a form of religion that was venerated by the mass of the people.

Greek genius was still prevalent in arts and in

literatüre. The Greek was the commercial lan guage of the empire, and it was Greek faith and learning that first disseminated the spirit of Chris tianity among the Gentiles. Had Christ appeared and announced his doctrines while the Greeks still adhered firmly to the spirit of paganism, where would have been the people, or the medium for disseminating his doctrines among the Gentile nations? Or, had he not appeared until the barbarians had destroyed the empire, and thus extinguished the genius of pagan civilization, what would have been the future of the people of Europe? That the announcement of the principles of Christianity at the culmination of paganism, was a happy coincidence for the perpetuation of civilization and the good of mankind, must, I think, be admitted.

Whether the spirit of religion under the guidance of pagan institutions, could have developed an ethical system that would have taught the individual to respect, love, and practice virtue, morality, and industry, not merely as a duty, but as a privilege to rise to a higher moral and intellectual life, and consequently to a higher state of civilization, it is now too late to inquire. Neither is it just to judge too harshly of paganism as a practical system of religion, since Christianity availed itself of its arts, literature, and philosophy, yet studied to avoid its theoretical fallacies and practical errors. Paganism had also discovered the necessity for, and developed the mode of forming religious and political organizations as a social basis. The great Author of Christianity announced not the first principle upon which to found religious or political organizations; religion as taught by Christ, was purely personal; while paganism had scarcely an existence independent of its legendary traditions. In Christ's omission to announce any special principles of religious organizations, or any special forms of public worship, there is evidence of his worldly wisdom. Had he denounced the then existing religious and political institutions, and urged an immediate reorganization of social economy, his doctrines would have died with him, or the social world would have suddenly been thrown into anarchy and confusion.

So eminently spiritual were his doctrines, that they found their way to the hearts of the seekers after truth, without producing scarcely a ruffle on the surface of society.

Nor is it strange that the first to believe in and to promulgate Christ's doctrines, should have been the very people that invented and developed pagan religion, arts, poetry, and philosophy. By nature speculative and inquisitive, they had exhausted every system of pagan metaphysics, yet had not reached as high a conception of deity, or of human morality, as that announced by Christ. Therefore it was very natural for the Greeks to become converts to the doctrines of Christ; yet in what manner this new faith was promulgated, or to what class it first appealed for converts, rests in obscurity.

"It would be singularly curious and instructive to trace, if it were possible, the rise and growth of any single Christian community, more especially that of Rome, at once in the whole church, and in the lives of the bishops, the first initiatory movements in the conquest of the world, and of the mistress of the world, by the religion of Christ.

"How did the church enlarge her sphere in Rome? How, out of the population (from a million to a million and a half), slowly gather in her tens, her hundreds, her thousands of converts? By what process, by what influences, by what degrees did the Christians creep onward toward dangerous, toward equal, toward superior numbers? How did they find access to the public ear, the public mind, the public heart? How were they looked upon by the government (after the Neronian persecution), with what gradations or alternations of contempt, of indifference, of suspicion, of animosity? When were they entirely separated and distinguished in general opinion from the Jewish communities? From what order, from what class, from what race, did they chiefly make their proselytes? Where and by what channels did they wage their strife with the religion, where with the philosophy, of the times? To what extent were they permitted or disposed to hold public discussion? or did the work of conversion spread in secret from man to man? When did their worship emerge from the obscurity of a private dwelling, or have its edifices, like the Jewish synagogues, recognized sacred fanes? Were they, to what extent, and how long, a people dwelling apart within their own usages, and retiring from social communion with their kindred, and with the rest of mankind?" *

From the obscurity of early Christian history, no conjecture can be formed regarding the spirit of its poetry and arts (if indeed it had any), prior to the time when they emerge from obscurity, and assume a public position as an independent religious organization; nor will the germs of Christian art appear until it has legends, and creates external symbols of its faith.

The spirit of asceticism which originated in the East, gradually extended itself throughout all Christian communities. Assuming the form of monasticism in Europe, it was the very antipodes of poetry and art; and the contest about creeds or

* Dean Millman's "History of Latin Christianity," Vol. I., p, 23.

formulas of faith, was also a serious obstacle to the growth and development of art.

The question of the Trinity was another source of agitation. Bishops anathematize and denounce each other in the vain attempt to effect a permanent organization, based upon a universal system of ethics. The exhaustion of pagan ethics, and the dissolution of the empire, disintegrated systematic currents of thought, denationalized the human mind, and left it an aggregation of individualities in search of a new central organization.

Nor will there be evidences of the development of Christian art until such organizations are formed as shall control and give direction to the currents of thought; nor until there are subjects and objects to symbolize, either legends of the past, or imaginative creations of the future, woven into a religious system of ethics, which shall guide and control religious organizations.

The current of our history naturally follows the Latin church, as it became the exclusive guardian and patron of Christianity in Europe, from its organization to the commencement of the Reformation. Yet without a slight notice of Greek Byzantine Christian art, the current of our history will be broken; as that is the connecting link between pagan and Christian art. We have no history of the erection of a Christian temple or place of worship prior to the building of the new capital; and to comprehend somewhat the condition of constructive art at that period, I refer the reader to Gibbon's description of the building of the new city, in the seventeenth and fortieth chapters of the "History of the Decline and Fall of the Roman Empire."

Its decline in arts had been even greater, if possible, than in politics and morals. Scarcely three centuries had passed from the full development of Roman art under the reign of Augustus, when the first Christian monarch found his empire too poor in genius and invention to adorn a Christian temple. Nor did the imperial mandate requiring the governors of provinces to establish schools for the training of ingenious youths in arts and sciences, restore, or even stay, the decline of pagan genius.

Now, if we view the history of the first three

centuries of the Christian era in the light of philosophy, in place of art, it may be possible to discover the causes of the decline of pagan genius and of morals. Assuming that Greek minds continued to control the genius of the age, it appears that in proportion as the imagination became exhausted in producing poetic and artistic imagery, it fell into the reflective mood, and thus gradually developed various systems of philosophy. Although Greek incipient philosophy was nearly as old as Greek art, yet, in its infancy, it exercised little influence outside the schools where it was taught; but as the spirit of poetry and art became exhausted, philosophy began to exercise an influence, direct, upon religion and government; and from the decline of pagan art to the rise of the Christian, philosophy becomes the medium through which we may trace mental aberrations.

During this transition, philosophy was chiefly confined to those countries and peoples which finally fell under the influence of the Greek church at the division of the empire. The culmination of Greek philosophy in the idealistic school of Plato, and in the sensualistic school of Aristotle, was the exhaustion of Greek genius in that direction; and thus the sensuous emotions and non-sensuous reason had passed through exhaustive processes, the one in ideal creations, the other in metaphysical speculations.

The exhaustion of Greek philosophy was manifest in its contact with Oriental mysticism, in the school of Alexandria. The mysticism of the East has ever appeared in that indefinite guise which has never announced a distinct system of philosophy, or originated a progressive system of theology. From the invention of symbolisms to the revelations of the prophet Mohammed, deity has been an "eternal mystery;" and, hence, every school of philosophy, or system of theology, that has come in contact with mysticism, has been baffled by the indefiniteness of its premises. Its very immobility has shielded it from exposure, and left its votaries to repose in the perpetual twilight of bigoted superstition.

The truth of this statement is demonstrated in its practical effect upon social and political organizations. With all its dreamy and mysterious speculations, it has never lifted the vail of ignorance from the minds of the mass of the people, nor shielded them from the oppression of unmitigated despotism.

The marked difference in the mental character of the Eastern and Western churches, and the one that has been prominent from their separation, is the speculative tendency of the former, and the practical tendency of the latter; the intellectual apathy of Asia, and the restless energies of Europe.

Says Dean Millman, "The East enacted creeds, the West discipline; the former reposed upon an effete civilization, the latter organized a progressive one."

Wherever Christianity spread among nations possessing arts developed in the service of a past history, and a developed system of religion, it of necessity modified those forms to conform to its own peculiar wants and necessities.

History furnishes no evidence of a new system of religion producing an original school of art original in spirit of ornamentation and principles of construction, in the midst of a school already developed. It will of necessity modify construction and ornamentation as it perfects its organization, and may thus, in time, become a distinct school; yet it will retain, in a certain degree, the elements of the school out of which it grew.

M. Taine, a modern French critic, says of St. Peter's of Rome, and the cathedral of Florence: 'They are the works of pagans in fear of damnation." However harsh and unexplained the remark may seem, there is more of truth in the suggestion than may at first appear. It is literally true, Christian art has never emancipated itself from pagan influences in Italy; and that is perhaps what M. Taine intended to express.

A description of some of the Greek churches may serve to illustrate more clearly some points of our subject. The term "Byzantine" has been given to the Greek Christian school of art, because it assumed the distinctive form of a school in the city of Byzantium, which has since received the name of Constantinople. Up to the time of the removal of the seat of the empire, by Constantine, from Rome to Byzantium, it is probable all Christian art—so far as there was any—was substantially the same.

From that time, however, there was a divergence; the Byzantine assuming more of the Asiatic in construction and ornamentation; while what is termed the Romanesque remained European in spirit, and underwent many modifications in various localities, in the transition from the Roman basilica to the transalpine cathedral.

In rebuilding the new capital, the Emperor Constantine greatly enlarged the boundaries of the ancient city, and adorned it with churches, palaces, theaters, porticoes, and aqueducts.

During the second and third centuries, art underwent a complete transformation from the post and lintel, to the pier and arch mode of construction; consequently, constructive ornamentation had become of secondary consideration in architectural design. The principles of sciography were superseded by the surface-painting of mosaics, colored marbles, frescoes, and gilding. So completely destitute of the higher power of artistic design was the age of Constantine, that he was reduced to the pitiable necessity of plundering the cities of his empire of their precious works of art—the products of the genius of a former age—to adorn his new capital. The wealth, the power, and the will of a monarch, may build a city, when his empire is too poor in genius and invention to adorn it. It is not the power nor splendor of monarchs that awaken the sensuous, poetic, and religious emotions in the bosom of man—the source from whence flow all artistic creations—neither can they arouse them from the lethargy of exhaustion and consequent demoralization, without unvailing new springs of life, from whence may flow a new faith, and thus create new hopes, aspirations, and desires.

The church of St. Sophia—the most noted of edifices of the Greek school—was founded by Constantine, in the year 325, and was re-built and enlarged by Constantius in 359. It was destroyed by a mob in 404, and rebuilt by Theodosius the Younger, in 415. It was again destroyed in a desperate riot and bloody strife between what was known as the blue and the green of the Hippodrome, in 532. Within forty days, Justinian relaid its foundations upon an enlarged plan, and completed the edifice within six years, substantially in the same form and style it appears at present.

The internal plan of the church foreshadows the Greek cross. Its principles of construction are similar to those of the basilica of Maxentius in Rome; and its dome and semi-domes are merely extensions of those constructive principles.

"The whole frame of the edifice was constructed with brick, but those base materials were concealed by a crust of marble; and the inside of St. Sophia, the cupola, the two larger and six smaller semi-domes, the walls, the hundred columns, and the pavement, delight even the eyes of barbarians with a rich and variegated picture. * * *

"The triumph of Christ was adorned with the last spoils of paganism; but the greater part of those costly stones was extracted from the quarries of Asia Minor, the isles and continent of Greece, Egypt. Africa, and Gaul.

"Eight columns of porphyry, which Aurelian had placed in the Temple of the Sun, were offered by the piety of a Roman matron. Eight others of green marble were presented by the ambitious zeal of the magistrates of Ephesus. Both are admirable in their size and beauty, but every order of architecture disclaims their fantastic capitals. A variety of ornaments and figures were curiously expressed in mosaic; and the images of Christ, of the Virgin, of saints, and of angels, which have been defaced by Turkish fanaticism, were dangerously exposed to the superstition of the Greeks."*

It is true, the interior of St. Sophia was decorated with mosaics, and there were images of historical characters whose names were venerated by professing Christians. Doubtless the early Christians had many speculative theories as to the nature or essence of the God-head, as men still have, yet that scarcely deserves the epithet "superstition," since the seeking for truth is neither superstition nor bigotry. Greek intellect was developed

* Gibbon's "History of the Decline and Fall of the Roman Empire." Vol. III., pp. 67, 68.

by the aid of polytheistic ideas; and while they may have truly believed in the doctrines of Christ, they still continued to reason with the same language, and in similar modes; that is, while they became Christians in faith and belief, they were still under the influence of the Alexandrian school of philosophy.

And the same may be said of their arts. Pagan art had been pregnant with anthropomorphism, and every human attribute had been represented as pertaining to a personal deity. And hence, when they decorated their Christian temples, from force of habit they could not stop short of personating the Saviour, saints, angels, and martyrs, the symbols of their faith and the legends of their church.

That these symbols were really objects of worship, no candid mind will scarcely believe. For if the Greeks had not passed the intellectual boundaries of image worship, they certainly would not have forsaken that splendid imagery of pagan mythology to follow so simple and comparatively unpoetic faith as that announced by Christ.

To personate in symbolic forms the object of veneration, was an educated habit, and, consequently, to a certain extent, a chronic mental development, — a physical necessity more than a moral depravity.

But since those mosaic images essayed to express moral and spiritual qualities more than physical action, they developed no architectural imagery or forms, no " marking and action of the muscles and the bones," but rather had a tendency to develop the art of painting. And it is perhaps to this feature of Greek genius that may be attributed the development of the Christian school of painting.

The legends ascribed to Christ, to the Apostles, to saints, and martyrs, were very different in spirit from those ascribed to the pagan deities; and hence, must have awakened very different images in the sensuous emotions. The former address themselves to man's moral and spiritual nature, and the latter chiefly relate to physical action.

Now, it is no great effort of the imagination to conceive, that to personate mental emotions of whatever nature, colors, light and shadow,—are more expressive than are the outlines of substance, whatever their forms and combinations may be. Hence, the spirit of pagan mythology tended to the development of sculpture and the forms of architecture; and Christian legends tend to the development of painting.

Consequently, there are but few original forms in Christian architecture; but many new combinations of forms and transformations of lines in the Latin school, but few in the Greek school.

Even the church of St. Sophia, with all its wealth of precious marbles, gilding, and mosaics, was externally anything but a beautiful, or even grand specimen of art. It has the appearance of the grouping together of a multitude of structures of irregular shape, size, and height, covered with broad shelving roofs, surmounted with a large flat central dome, with semi-domes surrounding its base.

The capitals of columns, and the ornaments upon cornices and arches, are a jumble of grotesque and fantastic forms, crowded together apparently without order or system, and in many instances used for the mere purpose of covering blank space.

In ornamentation, the Byzantine school tended toward the Saracenic school—doubtless the influence of the surrounding Mohammedan arts.

The church of St. Sophia may be taken as a fair example of the principles of construction, and style of decoration, of the Greek Christian school.

From the reign of Justinian, their structures appear to have diminished very greatly in size. The domes in the later edifices were elevated upon a cylindrical or polygonal drum, and there were frequently three upon the same edifice—a large central, and two lateral, of smaller dimensions. The principles of construction continued nearly the same throughout the school; while, in ornamentation, classical forms gradually disappear with every new series of structures. While the Byzantine school continued to approach nearer to the Saracenic in its decorative features, and even in general outline, it adhered to the round arch as a general rule; yet in the Saracenic school are to be found nearly every form of arch known to the building art.

The religion of the Greek church was introduced into Russia about the middle of the tenth century, and with it were introduced some of the elements of the Greek Byzantine school of art, engrafted on a local stock, which was in spirit Asiatic; thus presenting the singular phenomenon of a school of art compounded from two exotics.

The school is a strange jumble, yet it is an example of what will be the effect of the admixture of the elements of European with Asiatic art. Such a school may, perhaps, attract our curiosity, but it can never address itself to our affections or our intelligence, from the fact that Asiatic and European civilizations are too far differentiated to be made intelligible to each other; consequently, they become negative more than positive magnets, when united in one organization.

Such a hybrid may repeat itself, but it cannot organize into a progressive system. A progressive school of art can only spring from unity of faith and affection, with variety of sentiment, and gradation of abilities; it must have inception, growth, and development by variety of purpose, to give expression to subject and object.

ARTS OF THE LATIN CHURCH.

PART FIRST.

ARTS OF THE LATIN CHURCH.

PART FIRST.

How and by what means did Christianity overcome the influence of habits, customs, and organizations of paganism, with its splendid monuments of art, and its gorgeous ceremonials? How, little by little, did it usurp its power, and appropriate its wealth?

That the earliest contests between paganism and Christianity were moral, or questions of faith and practice, there can be little doubt. Perhaps the immediate successor of Christ proclaimed little else than the spirit of the doctrines which he had announced; yet with the gradual increase of the number of followers, there arose the necessity of organization; and to establish organizations upon a permanent basis, there must be established some common rules, or mutual agreements, by means of which the actions of each individual shall be guided and governed. This physical and moral necessity is the element of imperfection in all systems of religion. The more individual faith relies upon creeds, the less it aspires to spiritual regeneration. And yet it is difficult to conceive how the fruits of Christianity can be realized on earth, or civilization be achieved, without the aid of religious and political organizations. To accomplish this, individual minds must submit to discipline; religious organizations must have rules, acknowledged and obeyed, in like manner as political organizations have.

The earliest information we have of the Latin church, it had attained to an independent organization, with its bishops, priests, and deacons; existing separate and distinct from the mass of the people. Having attained to this position, it was prepared to make an open warfare upon the corrupt and licentious practices of paganism. The clergy assailed it with cutting sarcasm and bitter anathemas; not content with denouncing pagan worship, they discarded its literature, and declared its arts polluted with abominations of idolatry.

Thus pagan civilization was repudiated by the early Christians before they had developed a new school of arts or literature; and the human mind was doomed to grope its way for centuries, with no other guides than religious fanaticism and machinations of a sacerdotal aristocracy. The power of the clergy, temporal and spiritual, rose in proportion as the power of the emperors declined; the church sought to control society by first getting control of the human conscience, that it might control and shape to its own purpose an ignorant and undeveloped religious fanaticism. Yet the sequel will show that this was accomplished more by persuasive than by compulsory means. That it might effect its objects, the church organized societies, parishes, bishoprics, sees; established a uniform creed, a uniform mode of worship; and acknowledged one supreme head of the church, whose authority was acknowledged to be supreme above all temporal sovereigns.

The peculiar condition of society during the supremacy of the Latin church, not merely admitted of this assumption of arbitrary power, but absolutely required it.

Had the early Christian church in Europe been divided into a number of independent organizations, it could never have survived the conflict of social elements which raged during the decline, and for centuries after the fall of the empire. Nothing saved its integrity, and at the same time consolidated its power and extended its influence, except the imperative manner in which it enforced discipline, and obedience to its laws.

It is to be remembered, this power grew up when society was a chaos; when vast tribes or nations were traversing the Continent of Europe in pursuit of plunder, or in search of an inviting country to inhabit. And it was mainly through the influence of the church, the will and energy with which it pursued its purpose, that these disintegrated and contending elements were eventually cemented and consolidated into kingdoms and empires; it inspired the entire mass with the same religious faith, and taught it the first principle essential to form a civil government—obedience to the laws. It cannot, however, with truth be said, that that peculiar condition of the human mind was the effect of Christian principles. Since society was in a transition state, it was uprooting and expunging one system of religion and its attendant civilization, and implanting the principles of a new system of religion, and developing a new civilization.

Christianity moulded itself to the condition of things as they were, that it might guide and shape the undisciplined elements, through faith and hope, in the direction of truth. Christianity had to perform the double task of discarding pagan arts and literature, and to develop arts suited to the wants of its own peculiar institutions. Although the gorgeous and massive structures of pagan genius remained, yet they ceased to be objects of veneration, or even of utility. Sacrifices were no longer offered upon the altars of their temples, the amphitheaters had ceased to be places of public amusement, the conquest and occupation of the empire by the barbarians had nearly annihilated commerce, and the basilica was transformed into a Christian church.

Consequently, social organizations again assumed an infantile state, and entered upon the task of developing a new school of arts, to meet its special religious and social necessities, and inaugurate a new system of literature, to record events, and mark the eras and changes of sentiments and ideas as developed by its social, moral, and intellectual progress. Until society avails itself of these two main pillars of civilization, no decided progress can be achieved.

Perhaps the question may suggest itself, What was the necessity for discarding pagan arts and literature, since other systems must be inaugurated to fill their places?

This question can be answered intelligibly only by contrasting the arts of the two schools, since they embody the essence or spirit of the two religious systems.

It has been before stated, pagan art addressed itself chiefly to the senses, since its main objects were to exhibit the physical powers and beauties of the human form; it illustrated human passions and impulse by imitating physical action. Consequently, sculpture was its demonstrative art, and architecture its monumental or historical art. Painting became the demonstrative art of Christianity; it addressed itself to those faculties that are nearest allied to the moral sentiments; or, in other language, to the aspirations of the soul.

The Christian school of painting was inaugurated by essaying to illustrate the agonies of a crucified Saviour, the fortitude of a dying martyr, the mental agony of a repentant sinner, and depicted the legends of saints, of angels, the resurrection and the judgment; subjects wherein the body is present merely to personate the soul. Christ elevated religion above state; his doctrines were addressed to the heart, to the soul; they were not demonstrable by physics; he neither created, nor made use of symbols; his religious ideas did not rest upon legends of the past; they were founded upon man's relations to a just and infinite Being, and the relations of the finite with the infinite. Religion, as taught by Christ, was purely individual in its nature; its essence consisted in the thoughts, the hopes, the aspirations of the soul, and hence it required no special creeds; consequently, tended to no special organization, created no legends or symbols, and hence would have produced no arts. It might have had a poetic literature; but would neither have enacted nor recorded a history. So purely ethereal were the religious conceptions of Christ, that their essence cannot be embodied in substance, forms, or colors; neither can they be exhausted by language; consequently, no civilization can exhaust or rise above the ethical system founded upon pure Christianity.

Yet, all that pertains to man on earth is but mortal; and the doctrines of Christ, when left to less elevated and less spiritual natures, soon gravitated toward more material forms. His immediate followers became spiritual and social centres, around which the new converts gathered for spiritual instruction and mutual consolation and support; and thus were formed new religious and social communities.

The spiritual teachers of these communities

were their heads, and, consequently, soon became their governors.

The chief element in the life of the new community, is religious worship; and hence the first necessity to be supplied, is a place for worship; and thus the temple, the sacred edifice, again becomes the grand central figure in the social economy of the new community. But it is transformed—its objects are for internal use, not for external effect. Sensuous beauty had little influence in the affairs of the infant Christian church; the soul aspired to address itself to its Maker by the aid of its own spirituality, rather than through the medium of the senses. Yet structures of some sort were indispensable, and they found a convenient model in the Roman basilica; it was constructed for internal use, and it had not been defiled by the ceremonies of pagan worship. Whether any structure that had been used as a basilica, was actually consecrated to the sacred use of Christian worship, or whether new edifices were constructed upon the model of the basilica, we have no positive information. Nor is it very material to our subject, since we do not know that the first Christian churches constructed were modeled after the basilica.

It is not claimed that there was any special significance in the selection of the basilica as the model of the Christian churches. It occurred simply from this fact: the necessity for structures for public worship required that they should determine upon some model, and as there were but three models then known from which they could choose, namely, the temple, the amphitheater, and the basilica, they chose the latter, as it was the best adapted to their use.

It is both curious and instructive to compare the plans of Christian churches, from the fourth to the nineteenth centuries, and to see how the original plan has been substantially adhered to; which goes to prove that the great essential forms of Christian worship have not materially changed since its first organization. The primary objects of its church edifices have ever been the same, namely, to furnish a place for assemblage, whether large or small, where the people may assemble and unite as one person in offering praise and thanksgiving to the Author and Saviour of the world. Different creeds and rituals have caused slight changes in the mode of construction, and still greater variations in the system of ornamentation. But ornamentation is symbolism; and since faith and hope are passions and impulses independent of physical action, they cannot be symbolized. Consequently, there was no Christian art until there was a poetic history—legendary or literal—of what had transpired of a poetic or tragic nature, to the followers and founder of the Church of Christ.

This material necessity was gradually supplied by the church, as it increased in numbers and in wealth, and gradually receded, in time, from the tragic event which deified its great head and founder.

It kept gradually adding to its sacred calendar the names of saints and of martyrs, to each of which there were ascribed some miraculous or tragic legend. This embodied faith in action, and thus made poetic and tragic ideas demonstrable by substance, forms, and colors, or, in other words, created subjects demonstrable by symbolic language. And thus, we perceive, art is the interpenetrating of the actual with the ideal; the clothing of substance with poetic forms; the illuminating of the finite by a reflection of the infinite. It is a curious fact, however, that the Latin church made little or no progress in the arts until it entered upon its grand mission of propagandism among the barbarous nations of western and northern Europe.

There had no doubt been Christian churches constructed before that period, but they exhibit no originality of design or execution. The first indication of a regenerated genius appeared in that portion of Italy where the effete genius of the degenerate Romans was first enlivened by the youthful and vigorous blood of the Ostro-Goths and Lombards. All the barbaric tribes which spread over Europe during the first centuries of our era, professed to have some form of religion; but as they led a nomad life, they could not have had structures dedicated to sacred uses, nor even plastic arts; they were monotheists; their idea of God was, that he was the greatest of warriors;

and some tribes offered human sacrifices upon their altars. These semi-barbaric tribes may have had a legendary history, composed in poetry, and transmitted traditionally; but they had no symbols or demonstrative arts. Consequently, it did not cost them any great sacrifice of conscience or attachment to become converts to the church, since it was merely demonstrating by oral and visible symbols more clearly their own confused and undeveloped ideas of deity.

The great fact that they became adherents of the church, is sufficient evidence to warrant the above assertion; and that Christian art commenced to develop itself almost from the commencement of the amalgamation of barbaric tribes with the church, is also historically true.

Yet classic art has ever retained a certain degree of influence over the development of the arts of the Latin church east of the Alps; while west of them, Christian art developed an entirely original school. What is called Gothic,—yet should justly be called Christian,—art, never found its way into classic Italy in a pure form.

This phenomenon may find an explanation in the fact that the population west of the Alps was composed almost wholly of the tribes from Scythia and Scandinavia, while those which settled east of the Alps became amalgamated with the Roman people.

Neither were there any monuments of classic art west of the Alps to imitate, or to supply materials for construction of Christian churches. Consequently, Christian art took a more original form in Germany, France, and the British Islands, than in Italy.

The cause of this phenomenon may be two-fold: First, the absence of local monuments of art, which might attract the sight, and thus suggest a form which necessity might otherwise compel genius to invent, to embody in forms what the ideal had conceived. Second, it will hereafter be shown that the first Christian churches constructed in western Europe were erected by artists and artisans from Italy; yet these structures did not foreshadow the style of art which the Christian church was destined to develop upon a soil before unknown to art, and by the genius of a people before unknown to civilization.

There was nothing effete in the countries occupied wholly by the barbaric tribes—neither the monuments of a past civilization, nor the descendants of a people who had exhausted their genius in the development of a civilization that had culminated and declined. These youthful people had not passed the first stage in the development of civilization—the epic. Their life was a constant scene of strife; the heroic and the tragic formed a part of their daily life. The human mind, in such a state, is ever susceptible of new impressions, especially to that which relates to the marvelous or mysterious. And hence, the Christian missionary found a welcome among them, even in the depths of the Scandinavian forests. And as they had no organized system of religion, nor established forms of government, no arts or literature, there were few obstacles in the way of their accepting Christianity as a system of religion, and became adherents and supporters of the Catholic church. Consequently, the Catholic church became a part of every government organized by these primitive people—and hence her power and influence in Europe for many centuries. Her legendary literature became the *alma mater* of art. It was interwoven with every scene and incident of daily life. Even the very portals of heaven were described as adorned with the symbols of "Holy Church." While this magic influence extended over all Europe, yet it developed differentiated arts, in different localities, which can be explained only as the expression of different idiosyncrasies, and difference of soil, climate, and aspects of Nature.

Clovis, the founder of the French monarchy, was the first orthodox prince of barbaric origin. With the exception of the Franks, the barbaric tribes, at their conversion to Christianity, first gave their adhesion to the Arian creed. But with an alliance with Clovis, the Catholic hierarchy got perfect control of religious organizations in France. Yet there was very little progress made in arts, in France or Germany, until the reign of Charlemagne. The perpetual wars which prevailed between various nations, and between princes of the same nation, prevented any decided progress in civilization for several centuries after Christianity had become the universal religion of Europe. For self-protection, the church united the sword with the cross; nor did it hesitate to sanction the use of the former, to extend the rule of the latter. Charlemagne made Christianity the basis of his polity. Consequently, whatever was without the domain of the church, was equally an object of conquest as that which was without the temporal rule. Where his victories established civil government, there he also established the church; and the organization of his empire appeared complete when he had founded his eight great bishoprics. He also founded schools and monasteries for the encouragement and promotion of learning generally.

The extensive conquests of Charlemagne, his comparatively thorough, political, and religious organizations, gave an impetus to the building art by the large demands which it created for cathedrals, churches, monasteries, and for secular uses. But the attempt to revive literature proved to be premature; war was still the chief occupation of the superior class; nomadic habits had stimulated physical action, and mental action was dormant upon all subjects except war and religion. Literature, like art, is a thing of spontaneous growth, not a mechanical invention; nor is it in the power of man to will that art or literature shall grow, that can transpire only in the regular evolutions of nature.

There is a certain spirit of romance in the mental life of all youthful nations, all people just verging upon the first stage of civilization; a propensity to believe in the marvelous or miraculous; a certain credulity and desire for knowledge, which leads the mind to seek after hidden and mysterious truths. This mental phenomenon appears in the early history of every nation that has attained to a comparatively high degree of civilization. If we go back to the pre-historic period, we find it in the tents of the nomad races, upon the monuments of Egypt; it is prominent in the early history of Greece, and even in the early history of the Romans. And it was an active element in the life of the barbarous tribes that roamed over Europe for centuries before they became domiciled as agriculturists, mechanics, and tradesmen. Nor did it disappear with the first stage of civilization; religious zeal increased; the legends of the church were multiplied; poetic imagery is intensified in ideal conceptions; finally, ideality gradually develops actuality, in the form of poetry, art, literature, and science.

Thus, religion is the generative principle, the motive power, which develops the elements and laws of a progressive civilization. There may be religion without arts, and without civilization; but there can be no civilization without arts, neither can there be arts without practical religion. Consequently, all civilizations are based upon systems of religion. Hence their infancy, growth, maturity, culmination, and decline; and hence, also, the sad but moral and physical necessity of practical iconoclasm, in the form of religious and political feuds—wars foreign and domestic—to remove the barriers of ignorance, which a less intelligent, and less liberal age, has placed in the way of social and moral progress. The cause which necessitates this, is the extremes to which religious fanaticism and bigotry can lead the human mind before the imagination culminates in reason, when poetry and art yield for a time the supremacy to philosophy and science; and the idealist turns critic, analyzes the arts of the past, and compares them with the present, without perhaps taking into account the moral and intellectual difference of past and present society.

Yet there must be a certain degree of materialism in every system of religion, to develop either arts or civilization; arts must deal with substance, to embody its ideal creations; and so, civilization depends upon political, as well as religious organizations, for its development.

Now, while the Latin church exercised a great religious and moral influence over Europe, from the decline of the Roman empire until the barbaric races assumed something of a permanent political form, yet during that period very little progress was made in the development of art. The first glimmer of reviving genius was under the Ostro-

Goths in Italy. Yet, at first, it was little more than rude imitation of debased Roman art, a mixture of ornaments taken from Roman edifices, with original work, mostly imitations, with some feeble attempt at allegorical sculpture. During the eighth and ninth centuries, a much greater advance was made in Lombard Italy, to which a more minute reference will be made hereafter. But the first feeble attempt to execute a work of art in Germany and France, was during the reign of Charlemagne, whose greatness established a form of civil government,—which, however, relapsed into anarchy at his death. But his genius had left its impress upon society; the permanent foundations for the development of the feudal system were laid during his reign.

It does appear, feudalism was the first condition a barbarous and migratory people must assume, to enter upon a condition of life, that would develop civilization. While they were migratory, war and plunder were the chief occupation of the male population; property consisted chiefly in flocks and herds; yet when they became domiciled as agriculturists, mechanics, and tradesmen, land became the chief source of wealth; and as it became the property of those who had been the chiefs of the wandering tribes, so its control became the chief source of power under the feudal system. There were various ranks of feudal proprietors, the chief of which finally became king; to whom all others did homage, and rendered military service as compensation for the tenure of their fiefs. There were also many grades of the lower classes—those who tilled the land upon shares; serfs, or those who could not leave the estate upon which they were born; and the slave, who was the absolute property of his lord or master.

Feudal customs varied in different countries, yet its practical effect upon the development of social economy was substantially the same wherever it prevailed.

The church entered fully into the spirit of the system, became the proprietor of fiefs, had its villains and tenants at will. And thus the union of religious organizations with feudalism was the first distinct form which social and political economy of modern civilization assumed. These dual powers established—the church and feudalism working in harmony; the one to discipline mind, the other to organize and develop industry—barbarism was thus gradually crushed out, society cemented by mutual faith and community of interests, social progress was inaugurated, and humanity moved forward like a mighty rushing river, to work out its own destiny.

The church had taught discipline and obedience, and feudal servitude taught the necessity for industry,–the substratums upon which all governments rest, and without the aid and co-operation of which no civilization can be achieved. From this social condition there gradually came wealth, more than a fair proportion of which fell to the control of the church; and with this resource, and her influence over the minds of all classes, she grandly developes, step by step, little by little, change upon change, those series of ecclesiastical middle age structures, which so clearly portray the genius and peculiar mental development of the age in which they were conceived and executed.

Nor was constructive art confined exclusively to ecclesiastical structures during those ages; the feudal system originated and developed the feudal castle, which in its origin was both mansion and fortification, and from which, by a series of modifications, has come our modern palaces, mansions, villas, and even unpretentious dwellings. Yet all ornamentation of secular structures, in every school of art, is derived from the sacred school of ornamentation.

There is nothing of the imaginative or poetic in the study or composition of domestic economy, which can stimulate the imaginative faculties to the height of conceiving forms of beauty; legends of the supernatural, the miraculous, and the heroic, are the demonstrative subjects of art, whether in Egypt, Greece, Rome, or the Christian church; the cause and the source were substantially the same.

The legends of saints, martyrs, angels, the hosts of heaven, of the Latin church, stimulated and excited the imaginative faculties in a similar manner as did the legends of polytheism; only that the legends of the church were descriptive of that which pertains to man's spiritual nature, while polytheism chiefly described physical action; hence, the difference in the spirit of the systems of ornamentation which the two systems of religion developed. Utility also had its influence in the development of the two schools; the classic was eminently adapted to edifices for external effect, while the pointed Christian was as eminently adapted to edifices for internal use. Christian art in Europe took first the form termed Romanesque, under which term—for the sake of brevity—we will include all the round arch schools, since they do not vary so much in spirit as in degree of development, except that school which assumed a massive and symmetrical form in the hands of the Normans, in certain portions of France and the British Islands, and out of which sprung the pointed or Gothic school.

Now, the most inexplicable phenomenon in the whole history of art, is the evolution from the round to the pointed style; it can scarcely be called a new system of ornamentation, or a new principle of construction; nor was it the product of a new system of religion, or even a re-organization of the same system. It must have been caused by a more zealous enthusiasm than that which had ordinarily influenced the course of events, perhaps the natural sequence of the concentrated power of Catholicism, which had centered all mental action in the cause, and the extension of the power and influence of the church. Mr. Fergusson claims that "scarcely anything was done in pointed architecture which had not already been done in the round arch style," to which opinion I cannot subscribe; for the reason there is a certain material expression in the round style, that is not noticeable in the pointed style.

While it must be admitted the round styles reached a high degree of development in Italy, Germany, and some portions of France; yet, as sacred constructive art, it never did entirely rid itself of the secular expression which it received in its original development as Roman secular art.

But in the zenith of the concentrated power of the Catholic hierarchy, sensuous Christianity aspired to clothe its sacred temples with a more aspiring and spiritual expression. The full development of the pointed style was the culmination of sensuous Christianity; the reformation followed upon its full development. Its striking characteristic is its lofty aspirations; its spirit is ever expanding upward and outward; it aspires to make its portals broad enough to receive the world, and its spires lofty and light enough to reach heaven. It is the symbol of Christian faith, hope, and aspiration, in its simplicity and childlike credulity, when it rested in implicit faith in the bosom of Catholicism. Sensuous emotion invents legend upon legend, and ideal emotion creates symbol upon symbol, as it essays to illustrate the mysteries of redemption and salvation. The light of heaven sends its rays through every variety of beauteous forms, diversified by the most gorgeous colors, as it illuminates the sacred place of worship.

In no other school of constructive art can there be found the same extent and variety of ornamental forms, either externally or internally, nearly all of which were originally invented as symbols to illustrate some poetic or tragic legend, and hence their unique beauty. Whether the entire system of ornamentation of the pointed style was purely the outflow of sensuous Christianity, or whether foreign influences may have lent their aid, is at least an open question. One fact is historically true, the pointed style commenced to develop itself nearly simultaneously with the Crusades—which continued at intervals for about 175 years; and the pointed style was about 350 years in passing through its various evolutions, from its inception to its culmination and decline.

Now, there are many similar features in Christian pointed art, and Mohammedan Saracenic art, especially in the use of the pointed arch, which is of much earlier date in Asia than in Europe. There naturally arises the question, What influence, if any, had the Crusades upon the origin and development of the pointed style of ecclesiastical architecture? The era of the Crusades was one of great mental as well as physical activity, and during the early portion, at least, was almost wholly under the influence of the Latin church. Religious zeal and enthusiasm was the true cause of the origin and prosecution of the Crusades; and during that period there was also great enthusiasm in the construction of ecclesiastical structures. There is nothing in the structures erected during that period which indicates a servile imitation of any Mohammedan or Asiatic structure, and yet there is an indication of an inspiration of Asiatic poetry. During the Crusades, Europe and Asia met face to face—not merely as implacable foes, but in all their religious fervor, each with their peculiar temperaments, habits, dress, and manners. And especially were the scenes new to the European Christians. The holy sepulchre, and the cities that had witnessed the labors of the Apostles and early Christian converts, were enveloped in the artistic imagery of Oriental poetry and sentiment. That these scenes should have made an impression upon the sentimental minds of the pilgrims and crusaders is not strange; indeed, it would have been strange if they had not left their impress upon the sensuous emotions, in that sentimental age. Now, this may appear as far-fetched and overwrought; yet it cannot be denied that the era of the Crusades was one of great religious zeal and enthusiasm, and of rapid mental development. It was more imaginative, poetic, and artistic, than scientific or philosophic. The wars of the Crusades were conceived and carried on more in the spirit of enthusiasm than in deliberate and careful forethought of probable consequences.

Pointed art was the embodiment of the genius of the age in which it was developed, whether purely indigenous, or partially inspired by foreign causes. In its infancy, it was simple, massive, sparing of ornament, aiming at the grand rather than the beautiful. Yet, as its spirit gradually unfolded, its portals and windows were made broader and more elaborate in decoration; its vaultings were made more elaborate in the interlacing of its ribs and bosses; its pillars gradually became more slender and more numerous in its shafts and moldings; arches were first very sharp pointed, then gradually flattened into the equilateral, next the four centered, and finally sunk into the depressed. It has passed from infancy to youth, manhood, old age, and decay. The spring of life brought forth the flowers and the foliage; the summer developed the full-grown fruit; the fall ripened the fruit, and dried up the foliage; and the winter of exhausted genius congealed the sap, withered the stems, and left it a gnarled and lifeless trunk.

The sensuous life of a system of religion lives and moves in ideal symbolism, until sensuous genius exhausts itself; then written language supersedes symbolic forms, to delineate attributes, which leads the mind to reflection, comparison, and reason, and thence to mathematics and science; non-sensuous reason governs by fixed and determined rules and laws.

And hence, religious organizations cease to rest upon legends, and are based upon what reason conceives to be the laws ordained by Providence, or put forth by Christ, to govern the spiritual and temporal affairs of mankind; consequently, in the progress of human institutions, reformations are inevitable.

Sensuous Christian art culminated and declined

partly from the exhaustion of genius in that direction, partly from the introduction of mathematical rules; non-sensuous reason assumed the guidance of the human mind.

When Christian art culminated, it tended to secularization, in like manner as did Greek temple art in the second and third centuries of the Roman empire. But as Christian pointed art was more spiritual in its nature than Greek art, its elements could not be secularized to the same extent as could the Greek school.

Neither was its system of construction as well adapted to secular use as was the Roman; and hence, following the Reformation, came the revival of classic art, as well as literature and philosophy.

The pointed school of constructive art, was in essence purely impersonal; it was not composed to do honor to individuals, or societies, or to commemorate special events; it was the embodiment of the spiritual idea of the age in which it was developed, -the clothing of the temporal with the spiritual, -the aspiration to pass from the conditioned to the unconditioned, -to picture to mortals, in symbolic forms, the glories of the Immortal.

Constructive art in Italy, even in the service of the Latin church, did not rise entirely above the materialism of Roman art, out of which it grew; but sensuous Christianity in Italy developed a school of sacred plastic art, in the form of painting.

The sacred school of painting took its rise in Italy nearly simultaneously with pointed constructive art in western Europe, and doubtless both had their origin in the same cause—the religious enthusiasm of the age, guided and controlled by the concentrated power of the Catholic hierarchy.

The sacred school of painting was the product of that peculiar nature of Greek genius which gives individuality to all subjects and objects. It was this peculiar development of genius that covered the walls of St. Sophia, and other Greek churches, with pictures in mosaic, elucidating the legends of the Christian church in plastic forms, similar to the manner of depicting the legends of pagan deities.

And it was doubtless these mosaics that suggested the idea of stained glass in the pointed cathedrals—if they were not really the works of the same school of artists.

ARTS OF THE LATIN CHURCH.

PART SECOND.

ARTS OF THE LATIN CHURCH.

PART SECOND.

The paucity of historical records of early church edifices, renders a description of them very difficult in this age; and especially is it difficult to determine where the spirit of pagan art ceases, and where Christian art commences.

There was an apparent interregnum of creative genius from the decline of pagan to the rise of Christian art.

Taking the basilica of St. Peter as a fair example of the earliest Christian church edifices, we have a large, plain, five-aisled structure, lighted almost wholly from an inordinately high clear story, which was at that time a convenient mode of producing internal effect, in the absence of a systematic school of ornamentation. What ornaments were used, such as columns, cornices, corbels, were taken from the ruins of Roman edifices. In the construction of the roof, there is evidence of a fair knowledge of carpentry; and in the vaulting of the outer aisles, there is evidence of good constructive masonry; but there is an entire absence of the evidence of a genius capable of designing or executing a system of ornamentation.

What is known as a vestibule in our modern churches, was in the plans of the early churches an open portico—the narthex—where those penitents were admitted who were not in full communion.

Attached to some of the early churches, was a circular structure where the solemn rite of baptism was administered; and hence they took the name of baptistry.

In this general description of church edifices, it is not merely to point out the changes in plans and construction, but more particularly to note the gradual development of the various schools of ornamentation. In the construction of the series of basilican churches in Rome, there was a constant effort to resuscitate the classic orders, but in few instances with happy result. What had been originally created for external effect, could not happily be applied to internal use.

In the churches of Ravenna we discover the first effort of genius to emancipate itself from the influences of classic composition, and to subordinate its details to a new system of construction. Ravenna was the seat of the Gothic kings, and under their reign the new development was inaugurated.

The exterior of the church of St. Apollinave ad Classen is a plain structure, presenting a uniformity of design, ornamented with a series of flat pilasters supporting semi-circular arches. The walls of the clear-story were nearly as high as the outer walls of the aisles; the roofs were a moderate pitch. The internal supports of the clear-story were round columns supporting semi-circular arches; the ornaments were rude imitations of classic details.

Attached to this church was a round tower, with high base, and eight stories of superstructure; the two first with very small single windows; the third and fourth, large single windows; the fifth, couplets;

the sixth, seventh, and eighth, triplets. It was crowned with a heavy projecting cornice, and low pitched roof. It is not so clear, what was the peculiar use of this tower, since it is generally believed bells did not come into use until some centuries later.

This peculiar school passed through several developments, and reached its culminating point in the cathedral of Pisa. It did not fully overcome the influences of the Roman arcade school. The cathedral of Pisa is literally covered with a series of arcades, without special regard to uniform distribution on front or flank, nor of the arches of the different stories, which would be very offensive were they not so large in the lower series, and so comparatively small in the upper series. The details are not sufficiently massive to produce grandeur of effect; yet the variety of forms in the composition produces a picturesque and pleasing effect.

There was a class of circular structures, belonging to this school, which were clothed with a sacred character; yet, judging from their peculiar construction, their objects must have been more liturgical and memorial, than merely as places for public worship. Nearly all of this class of structures were quite plain upon the exterior; some were equally plain upon the interior. Symbolical allegory appears to have been sought in plan, construction, and ornamentation, especially in such structures as St. Vitale, at Ravenna, and St. Lorenzo, at Milan.

The Lombard school was a decided remove from the Roman basilica. Its chief characteristics are the upward tendencies of its principal dividing lines, and the development of the central tower. The plan of St. Antonio, at Piacenza, fully develops the Latin cross; and at the junction of the nave, transepts, and choir, there is a central octagonal tower, of uniform size the entire height, divided into four sections, the three upper with coupled windows. The tower is capped with light cornice, and low, pitched roof. The structure is simple, and without pretense of ornament, either external or internal. Yet this school furnishes many samples rich in picturesque designs; and among these may be mentioned the church of St. Michael, Pavia, which has a tall and gracefully-tapering tower, a highly decorated apse, and the interior exhibits the grouping and clustering of pillars as internal supports, which have superseded round columns; and groined vaultings have taken the place of timber roofs, or flat, plastered ceilings.

The front of the cathedral at Piacenza presents some marked and original features. It is divided into three parts, having flat angle buttresses, and two flat centre buttresses, extending to the lower member of the arcade parapet, which crowns the structure in a pediment form. It has three projecting porches covering the doorways, the central considerably larger than the lateral ones, all of which are two stories in height.

Over the central porch is a large central window, filled with elegant tracery; while over the lateral porches there runs an arcade belting of moderate height; and above this, on one side, is an immense clock face, while the other side is a blank wall. This cathedral has a high square tower of uniform size, flat buttresses upon the angles, and a flat centre buttress upon each face, all terminating under the lower belt of the upper section, which is an open arcade about half the width of the tower in height. The tower is crowned with a short conical spire.

The front of the church of St. Zenone, at Verona, is a still nearer approach to an independent and original style. It presents three divisions, the centre one slightly projecting, and higher than the lateral divisions, terminating in a pediment form, and the lateral divisions terminate in half pediments. It has one grand central entrance, covered with a light, elegant porch, above which is a large circular window, with bold but simple tracery. The lateral divisions have heavy buttresses upon the outer angles, and each space is divided into four parts by slender buttresses, which terminate under the cornice, and also serve as corbels for the scalloped frieze, which is one of the marked features of this school. About midway in height, on the lateral divisions, there is a horizontal belt of open arches, in height about one-sixth of the whole height of the lateral divisions.

The front of the cathedral at Zara is a still more original example, with more unity and harmony of design. It presents three divisions, the centre one slightly projecting, and rises moderately above the lateral divisions, terminating in a regular pediment. The lateral divisions also terminate in half pediments. The first story is high, with plain walls, has three grand portals ornamented with shafts upon the jambs, and bold mouldings upon the arches. The second story is a blank arcade, extending in height to the eaves of the lateral divisions; the third and fourth stories of the central division have circular windows with tracery of a similar pattern. The one in the fourth story is considerably smaller than the one in the third, as the former is chiefly located within the triangle of the pediment. The outlines of this structure are simple, bold, harmonious, and effective, and exhibit more freedom of conception and originality of composition than any structure heretofore described. It certainly indicates the presence of a youthful genius.

The German round school, in its general composition, made vertical lines more prominent than horizontal lines, by breaking the body of the structure into various parts, grouping towers of various forms, sizes, and heights, and crowning them with spires, gables, and high pitched roofs. This school fully developed the spire as a crowning member of a tower.

The churches of the Apostles and St. Martin's, at Cologne, have the peculiar picturesque feature of an open arcade under the eaves of the apse and central tower. These two churches present great regularity of parts and harmony of detail, which consist externally of flat or half round buttresses supporting arches, light horizontal belts, light eave cornices, and high pitched roofs.

Perhaps the most interesting structure in the round German school, is the church at Larch. It is regular in the outline of its plan, and harmonious in its details ; but is rendered very picturesque and effective by the various heights of different parts of the structure, and the harmonious grouping of the towers with the main structure.

Its vertical lines decidedly prevail over its horizontal lines; and while it has no feature which belongs strictly to the pointed school, yet there is a poetic quaintness in its expression which is nowhere seen in the schools which preceded it. The German round school was the most poetic of all the schools which preceded the pointed.

In the south of France we find a school which in style of decoration is similar to the Byzantine; and while the constructive principles are substantially the same, the outlines of the plans are materially different. They are usually cruciform; many are without aisles or clear-stories, are long and narrow, divided internally in squares, each of which is vaulted in the form of a dome. But the peculiar feature of the churches in the southern provinces of France, is the great variety in the outline of the plans, and style of decoration.

The church of St. Front, Perigeux, in style, is a fair example of the Byzantine school; while the church of St. Sernin, Toulouse, is a fair example of the modern Italian style of church architecture.

The church of St. Eloi, at Espalion, is a fair sample of the German school of the ninth and tenth centuries; the church at Loupiac is a good example of the round Norman school, while the church of Notre Dame, at Poitiers, exhibits all the features of the Norman school as it was about passing into the pointed style.

The Norman was the most massive, the most impressive, grand, and solemn, of all the round arch schools.

The purest specimens of this school were in Normandy and England. It was the prevailing style in Normandy at the time of the Conquest, and hence its introduction into England. The peculiar features of this style were very massive walls, flat or half round buttresses extending from base to eaves the same size, cornices light, high pitched roofs, windows usually small, doors moderate size, deep sunk into the walls, jambs and arches elaborately ornamented with shafts, and mouldings, with chevron and tooth ornament.

The towers were usually large, low, very massive, and usually without spires.

Many of the early Norman churches were doubtless constructed with the view of serving as a place of defense, in case of sudden emergencies.

Now, if we turn to the East, the birth-place of the arch, we find that it has assumed an infinite variety of form, to give expression to that unuttered poetry which has ever held the human mind a slave to ignorance and superstition. Its dreamy and contemplative asceticism has relieved the inertia of its nature, by its imaginative creations only. It has never descended to the practical, where sensuous emotion divides the domain of intellectual and moral action with non-sensuous reason, where the labors of both are brought into requisition for the good of society.

In the more temperate climate of Europe, however, the creative energies have taken precedence of the mere imaginative; physical necessity being a stronger stimulus to action than poetic asceticism. Where there is physical action, there will also be mental action; but where physical necessity is the cause, the imagination will be held in check by the practical, just in proportion to the pressure of the physical necessity, or according to external influences. Consequently, in temperate climates, the imaginary productions will be in proportion as man triumphs over nature, since they must relate to the practical.

Such productions can never be mere poetic fancy, but must embody the spirit and sentiments of religious and poetical organizations.

Hence the superior qualities of European art, as compared with Asiatic. For, as we see, when the creative takes the precedence of the imaginative or reflective, society is at once relieved of its inertia, and progress is inevitable.

When, however, the reflective takes precedence of the creative, society makes little or no progress. Art aims merely at the suggestive; it cannot rise to the condition of a progressive school.

But to its mere imaginative creations there are no limits, save the feebleness of human intellect. It wanders everywhere, and centres nowhere, creates without a purpose, and applies without effect. Deity is not a creative power, but an all-absorbing essence, leaving nothing for the energies of man but the contemplation of the final annihilation of all individuality in the Eternal Unity. Hence Oriental art is as vague in its expression as its name is poetic, and Europeans who look upon it only realize its unintelligible character, and it is this mainly which makes it of any special interest to a Christian. It teaches him practically little or nothing; but it presents to his imagination a new world of poetic imagery. Now, it is not a very wide stretch of the imagination to conceive the pointed school of art to be the work of the Germanic races of Europe; their own social necessities dictating the mode of construction, while its ornamentation was conceived under the influence and stimulus of the poetic sentiment of Oriental art. For we must not forget the fact that Oriental art gave almost every conceivable form to the arch, the grand feature of the pointed style; and further, that it is much easier for a people to become captivated with a foreign poetic sentiment, than to adopt a constructive system that is not in harmony with their established institutions. Intellectually, we are ever in pursuit of novel ideas and new poetic imagery, while we are ever averse to those ideas which immediately effect the status of our social organizations, and it is in the pursuit of the former that we unconsciously work out the changes in the latter.

It was in the heart of France, where the crusaders had been the most numerous and enthusiastic, that pointed art first assumed the forms and importance of a distinct style. The round Norman was first relieved of its massive character by the substitution of the pointed in place of the round arch.

The broad, flat buttresses assumed a bolder and more prominent form, and in place of sloping into the wall, or finishing with the cornice, they terminated in a graceful pinnacle above the eaves of the roof, thus completing the triumph of vertical over horizontal lines. The high pitched roof which capped the principal tower, shot up into a tall and graceful spire.

The round arch ceilings of the interior were superseded by highly ornate pointed and groined vaulting, with sculptured bosses clasping the intersecting ribs. And to relieve the walls of the clear-story from the lateral thrust of the inner vaulting, the flying buttress was introduced, with its base resting upon the outer wall of the aisle, and its crown against the wall of the clear-story, and terminating in a graceful finial, which broke the monotonous sky-line of the roof. The massive piers which supported the clear-story were changed to graceful ornate clustered pillars, with moulded base and foliated capitals.

The massive walls were diminished in thickness as the projection of the buttresses was increased; and the window openings were enlarged as the richness and intricacy of its tracery were developed.

These are the principal modifications which were made in the constructive systems; yet slight as they at first appear, they changed the entire expression of the edifice.

But a more spirited and radical change was effected in the system of ornamentation. It appears like the expansion of ideas as from a sudden inspiration.

The edifice appeared to expand into new life, like a forest in the spring season, which is just putting forth its foliage and blossoms, to gradually develop to maturity, ripen into a golden autumn, and gradually decay.

It would be tedious as well as unprofitable to attempt an explanation of the gradations in the rise and decline of the pointed school, without a series of illustrations, which is beyond the present design of this work.

But, to describe its development in a figurative sense, the internal, nervous energy of sensuous emotion has thrust out upon the surface the bones of the Etruscan school; and they compose the constructive elements, in the form of bold, projecting buttresses, towers, pinnacles, flying buttresses, piers supporting arches, spires reaching toward the heavens; and, internally, clustered pillars, clear-story arches, groined ceilings, corbels, and pendants.

The muscular action of the Greek school no longer binds the fabrics together by continuous horizontal bands, but is concentrated around window and door openings in the shape of delicate moldings, congeals into delicate tracery in window heads and on canopies of niches, gathers into knots in the form of corbels, crockets, and finials, twines around the bases and capitals of pillars, spreads over the surface of clear-story arches, and clings to the angles of the vaulted ceilings. In a word, wherever the artist touches his pencil, there he leaves the impress of his nervous sensuous emotions. Bones, muscles, nervous energy, all aspire to make the temple a fit dwelling-place for the living God, as the type of the temple itself is the tenement of a living soul.

English authors have divided the pointed school into three periods, and have applied the terms, early English, decorated English, and perpendicular English. This is perhaps proper for Englishmen; but it is too local for Continental Europe or America, for the reason that the terms would seem to imply that the style had its origin chiefly in England, which is not the fact. These divisions are also entirely arbitrary, since there are no distinctly marked periods in the development of the school, but each successive series grew out from each other in a more ornate and intricate system of ornamentation. And in this, it was not different from other schools that have been noticed. To illustrate all the features of the style minutely, however, the divisions are a decided convenience, and, from this point of view, are very properly recognized.

The early English dates from about 1180 to about 1300; the decorated, from 1300 to about 1380; and the perpendicular, from 1380 to about 1540. If these divisions were to be applied to the French school, the dates would require to be some years earlier, thus showing that the French preceded rather than followed the English school.

While the poetic spirit of pointed art was one throughout Europe, yet there were many shades of variation in plan, construction, and decoration, which is to be attributed to the peculiar idiosyncrasies of different nations, and to local influences, more than to any decided difference in the spirit of Christianity, or of outward forms of worship.

If we compare the French and English schools,

we find that in plan the French cathedrals are much wider in proportion to length than the English; that their choirs usually terminate in a chevron; that is, there are a number of semi-circular chapels arranged around the semi-circle of the choir; while the English choirs usually terminate in a square recess, and frequently with what is termed the lady chapel, beyond the chancel proper. Another feature in the plan peculiar to the French, is placing the walls of the aisles upon a line with the outer line of the buttresses, thus forming a series of small recessed chapels between the buttresses on each of the inner sides of the cathedral.

The French cathedrals are much higher internally, in proportion to their length, than the English. The grand idea of internal effect in the French cathedrals appears to have been height; while in the English, it appears to have been length.

The western were the principal fronts, and the French cathedrals are marked for their broad, lofty, and highly ornate portals, above which are the great circular windows, with their gracefully-flowing tracery; while the western fronts of the English cathedrals have usually low portals, above which are the five and seven great bay-windows, with heads of beautiful tracery. In spirit of design, the French school appears more poetic, and has greater freedom of imagination; while there is more of the mathematical and conventional in the English school.

As for the idea that the pointed school of art owed its origin and development to the genius and learning of the Freemasons: the difference in design and execution of the various local schools, is evidence that they emanated from a genius less trammeled by arbitrary conventionalities than those which governed the organizations of Freemasons. It is a fallacy to suppose that any special class, or local community, could produce a school of art that was the grand feature of the age; it is the universal religious spirit of the age that produces such a school.

Founded in the religious zeal of the twelfth century, the pointed school commenced its development without apparent fixed laws of proportions, or organized system of ornamentation; the pure offspring of the imagination. Ignorance, according to the common usage of the term, was too general in the twelfth century to found a school of art upon mathematical principles, were it possible so to found a school.

In its middle life, however, it gradually assumed forms and proportions consistent with fixed laws, which eventually assumed the control of its development, and it finally culminated in a series of mathematical and geometrical forms, beautiful in themselves, but devoid of the spirit of sensuous emotion or creative genius.

The French historian, Michelet, asserts Gothic architecture to be purely the offspring of the imagination, yet insists it was developed under fixed laws, which culminated in the cathedral of Cologne.

His theory is, that every Gothic structure has its numerical standard, which, with its subdividers and multipliers, are the guiding measures for the whole structure.

Now some laws, when applied to the later works of the school,—as the cathedral of Cologne,—might hold true, as they would when applied to the later works of any school; but that such laws are recognized in their infancy, I believe to be fallacious. The imagination is more vivid in youth than at mature age, and although genius may retain the mind in that solvent state when it is ever susceptible to new impressions, yet method is essential to success in practical life. Consequently, the more the imagination is subjected to the practical, the more it is guided by reflection, and reflection moves by the law of numbers.

Reason, therefore, assumes the mental guidance, as genius exhausts the imagination, and art culminates in a series of mathematical rules; and as reason neither creates nor destroys, art and society remain comparatively stationary while purely under its control.

But as the necessities and desires of society are constantly changing its exterior surface, so must art change in its forms, while its spirit may be that of the past.

The concentrated energies of society upon some special idea cannot fail to mark the age by signal results ; yet its solidarity, under the accumulated weight of the creations of its genius, often proves a serious obstacle to social progress ; yet the products of the human mind under such influences are of the very highest order of special truths, which, when carefully studied, greatly aid in the comprehension of the true elements of art. Whenever society concentrates its energies upon some special religious idea, the arts become the mediums by which it gives outward expression to its internal sensuous emotions. But its development and the progress of society is what eventually works its degradation, by its application to common-place purposes, without due discrimination, or proper application.

ARTS IN THE UNITED STATES.

ARTS IN THE UNITED STATES.

So far as our school of constructive art had an original prototype, it was the log cabin invented by our "Pilgrim Fathers." The hut or wigwam of the aborigines has had no more influence upon the development of our school of constructive art, than had the tents of the nomads, or the huts of the aborigines upon the development of the Egyptian, Greek, or Roman school. The primary object of the log cabin was utility, constructed of trunks of forest trees, either round or squared. The nature of the material, and the use for which the cabin was designed, did not admit of ornament. It was not attempted, perhaps not desired.

The facts are, constructive art was at a low state in Europe when emigration first commenced to flow toward the continent of America. Europe was still in the convulsive throes caused by the

Reformation; the Catholic Church had exhausted the genius of sensuous emotion in depicting its legends in forms and colors; the human mind became less credulous and more inquisitive; non-sensuous reason began to assert its right to investigate the nature of evidence. For the Reformation was an effort to place reason on a level with a faith that was put forth when the human mind was incapable of reasoning, and thus emancipate the mind from the oppression of a bigoted tyranny.

The tendency of the Reformation, at first, was to make religious faith entirely analytical, leaving synthesis entirely out of the question. Hence, the rapid disintegration of the new religious organizations, and the formation of new sects; and hence, also, the decline of art during the period of the Reformation. Yet during that period there was great intellectual activity. Philosophy and science made great progress; that is, the ascendency of abstract theology was broken, and other mental subjects assumed their proper status. Theology fell into metaphysical disquisitions, and thus exposed itself to philosophical criticism, and still severer criminations and recriminations by its own professors. And this was the mental and moral condition of the human mind, when our ancestors chose the wilderness of America for their future home, that they might enjoy religious liberty, and also exercise the privilege of persecuting those who might presume to differ with them in belief upon the subject of theological dogmas. Yet it is unjust to ridicule or to criticize too harshly our ancestors, since they were a bold, laborious, and, as I believe, a conscientious race of men. Whatever they may have been guilty of, they never uttered so monstrous a heresy as to declare human slavery a Divine institution. The burning of witches may indicate a religious insanity; but the declaration that God created one race of men to be the slaves of another race, exhibits a state of moral depravity of which history furnishes no parallel, for the reason the Christian church had declared all men "equal before God;" and if that be true,—and we dare not dispute it,—they must be equal before the law, for our laws are founded upon Christian ethics. Now, while the church had proclaimed this humane doctrine, yet, it must be admitted, professing Christians did not always observe it, nor did the authorities of the church punish those who violated it. This apparent inconsistency in the practice of the church has its explanation in the fact that the spirit of modern slavery had its origin in the terrible wars between the Christians and Mohammedans, and each contending party indulged in the inhuman practice of reducing their prisoners of war to perpetual servitude.

Yet this much should be said in extenuation of Christians: they were not the first aggressors, but stood on the defensive, fought for self-preservation against the wild fanaticism and grand scheme of propagandism, by conquest and subjugation, of all who would not become disciples of, or pay tribute to, the prophet Mohammed. Nothing could repel such an unscrupulous fanaticism, except another equally zealous and determined; and this the church had the influence to inspire in the minds of its followers. And as the church was growing in power and increasing in numbers, while Mohammedanism was passing through a succession of dynasties,—each succession apparently more weak and effeminate,—the church finally assumed the aggressive, and perpetuated those monstrous frauds upon the credulity of its followers, the wars of the Crusades.

The completion of the wars of the Crusades was the culmination of the centralized power of the Catholic church. The Crusades had caused great mental as well as physical action; had presented new and novel scenes in outward, as well as inner life, which had given rise to comparison and reflection, and had thus emancipated the human intellect from the despotism of a centralized theology.

Following this, modern commerce took its rise, and modern slavery assumed its second phase; it became an article of merchandise to gratify the cupidity of man. In this condition it found its way to the infant colonies of America; where, after undergoing various social and political modifications, it finally assumed its third and last phase, the basis of a political organization, for the purpose of controlling the governmental policy of the nation. This was its culminating point; it had assumed a position where it must check the growth of liberal ideas, or destroy itself in the effort. We have the final result.

Christianity has destroyed the evil which it created in the dark hour of its trial, and has thus vindicated its integrity, when it declared "all men equal before God;" and the great republic has finally vindicated its integrity, when it declared "all men equal before the law." And thus we see human slavery was like all human institutions; it must control whatever it came in immediate contact with, or must itself decline, either gradually by toleration, or rapidly by violence.

Thus there has been two diametrically opposite social systems expanding side by side, for a time apparently harmonious and without envy or malice, but the sequel has shown that there was a reservation of purpose which was not exhibited upon the surface, but waited "the logic of events" to fulfil its destiny.

Now, if we analyze these opposite social systems,

it will readily appear that the longer they existed, the greater the divergence, and consequently the more irreconcilable they became. Slavery grew constantly more arrogant, ignorant, and inhuman, from the immoral and brutal practices which it tolerated.

Public education was neglected, and in some localities prohibited; the practice of whipping degraded the slave to a level with the beast, while it made the master indifferent to human suffering.

Christianity was degraded to the condition of teaching the slave obedience to his master, and either voluntarily or by compulsion remained domiciled with this inhuman institution, witnessing its degrading practices without condemnation or even censure.

Where are the evidences in such a community of the spontaneous elements, the ideal sensuous emotion, or the active non-sensuous reason, that expands to the creation of art, literature, philosophy, and science? It must be admitted they possessed these inherent qualities, but the influences of slavery prevented their development; and with out some foreign source from which to draw the elements essential to perpetuate civilization, slavery would have lapsed into utter barbarism within the life of three generations.

Now, if we turn to the early history of the colonies of the free states, we find the moral anomaly of religious persecutions, excessive zeal in the advocacy and defense of special creeds, the tendency to disintegration of religious organizations, and the frequent appearance of new sects. If this mental condition did not tend to immoral practices, it certainly did encourage the belief in infidelity. Infidelity is not the normal condition of the human mind, as all men must believe in something,— since they cannot believe in nothing. Consequently, all religious controversies about the nature of Deity, and the attempt to define the special laws he has decreed to govern the acts of all mankind, will always develop a certain amount of what is termed infidelity; for the reason, all men cannot see the will of God expressed in that special manner; yet none can fail to see the outward manifestation of his actual existence in the works he has created. This apparent anomaly in the phenomena of the human mind, simply arises from the imperfections of man.

It was the grand disintegration of human belief under the patronage of Catholicism, which awakened the first aspirations for religious and political liberty in Europe; and it was the failure of any one particular sect or denomination to secure the entire control of the religious community, that has secured to us religious liberty. Unity of belief upon the great principles of Christianity, and diversity of sentiment upon its practical details, are essential to secure religious and political liberty. The former guarantees the integrity of the state, and the latter guarantees the freedom of individual opinion.

There does not appear in the infantile life of our nation, anything specially marvelous or poetic. The legends of our early religious belief were composed chiefly by theological pugilists.

The true cause of the absence of the legendary and poetic in our early history, may be attributed to the mental development of the early colonists, who had already passed through that historic stage; and hence, they reared the school-house simultaneously with the church edifice, thus laying the foundations to perpetuate religious and political liberty, which they had achieved "through great tribulation." The perpetuation of our political liberties are as dependent upon our common school system, as our religious liberties are úpon the perpetuity of the right of individual belief.

An intelligent belief is the only religious belief that can secure community from the despotism of a hierarchy, since religious organizations are essential to all conditions of civilization; to escape from the despotism of arbitrary creeds and rules, individual belief must rest upon a certain development of the reasoning powers. Or, in other language, philosophy or human reason has a tendency to repudiate the special dogmas of theology, not for the purpose of denying the truth of the great essentials of Christianity, but for the purpose of rising to higher generalities of relative truth.

For what purpose would philosophy deny the

great truths announced by the founder of Christianity? If philosophy does not accept the ideas of Deity as put forth by some system of religion, it must put forth its own ideas; for without the belief in the existence of a supreme Being, or an intelligent First Cause, man cannot reason at all; that is, to deny the existence of an intelligent first cause, to whom may be referred all phenomena, is to negative all reason.

Hence, religious emotions are the primary elements in all mental development; but if it continues the supreme and arbitrary ruler in all things, progress, or mental and moral development, will soon cease, from the fact that man possesses other mental faculties than those which spring from ligious emotions.

It is in the infancy of life, either national or individual, that religious emotions are most vivid; and it is in this mental state that sensuous emotion gives outward expression to its highest and noblest ideal conceptions in forms of art creations. These are the spring flowers of mental life, which gradually develop the fresh fruits of history, and eventually ripen into literature, philosophy, and science, at more mature age. Not that art retires from the field of intellectual action as other branches of mental pursuit come gradually forward, but with each evolution it becomes less sensuous, and more practical; with the development of social economy, it gradually descends from the ideal to the useful. When art is confined to purely sacred subjects, it may be considered in its homogeneous state; and it passes to the heterogeneous, as it diffuses itself in works of a more secular nature, and for various purposes; yet the sacred always remaining the fountain head, from the fact that art, in the abstract sense, is purely emotional or ideal, and receives its highest practicable types when demonstrating ideal subjects. Consequently, as constructive art passes from the sacred to the secular, from ecclesiastical to domestic, it does not develop original forms as in the ideal school, but gradually modifies those developed in the ideal school, to give a proper expression of purpose to domestic structures.

Religious ideas had no infancy in America, and

hence art was "cheated of its birth-right," all its primary elements of decoration were drawn from foreign sources, and engrafted upon a constructive system chiefly of our own development, and thus our school of constructive art has become semi-indigenous.

There is nothing mythical or legendary in our early history which can be symbolized in forms of constructive art, from the simple fact that the mind passed beyond that point of development before we began as a nation to enact history. Therefore, the only true mode left to us, to develop a correct national school of constructive art, is to conform our constructive system to the strictest rules of utility, and decorate them with those forms which harmonize with, and clearly express, the purposes of the structure, and thus our constructive art would truthfully express our national development. The taste and judgment of the professional architect in this country, is adaptation of plan to purpose, and of style to material and to locality. In this sense he displays correct taste and sound judgment, or poor judgment and bad taste, in the same sense as does an author, or an orator, in the selection of language to illustrate their subjects.

In the creative schools, the artist doos not exercise this semi-sensuous reason so much as a vivid and creative imagination; but in all such schools, ornamentation is of primary, and utility of secondary consideration. But there are no schools at the present day that can be said, in the strict sense of the word, to be creative. Yet the artists of the Old World have the monuments of the creative schools before them, which are greatly superior to books or prints as a study, since they serve to strengthen and confirm the judgment, as well as suggest forms of beauty, and harmony of proportions.

These monuments are objects of veneration to the mass of the people; which tends to develop a correct taste, and furnishes a certain amount of knowledge, and in this the artists of Europe have decidedly the advantage of those in America. But if we have not the monuments of a past age in our midst as a study, we are, or ought to be, free from the temptation of selecting models which served the wants and necessities of an obsolete age, and applying them to modern uses. And the practice would be the more reprehensible in us, since our institutions, domestic habits, and customs, are further removed from middle age customs and habits, than are those of modern Europe. Hence, if we adhere to the only true principle of modern constructive art, we may yet develop a school that shall equal, if not rival, in correct taste and sound judgment, any school yet developed. The field for operation is large, and the obstacles in the way of achieving the desired end are comparatively few; the greatest of which is, the general ignorance upon the subject, from the fact of the want of proper monuments as a study for the public, as well as the artist. But we shall never develop a correct public taste by selecting models from obsolete schools, and applying them to our own uses; for the reason, opinions have changed upon the subjects of religion and government, and consequently upon the subject of social economy, more especially in America than in Europe; and unless we desire to effect a retrograde movement in the evolutions of human life, we should not adopt literally what the past has produced; for that is accepting its vices with its virtues; yet we may imitate the beauties of its art creations; we must accept its spirit, but we may leave the dead carcass of its faults and imperfections to rest in peace.

Protestantism should have "conscientious scruples" about adopting entire the form and structure of a Catholic church; strip it of its legendary symbols of saints and martyrs, its shrines, its high altars, its confessionals, the very spirit and essence of its speciality, and consecrate it to Protestant worship; for the reason, the forms of worship are different; the edifice was conceived, constructed, and decorated, to harmonize with and accommodate one form of worship, but not the other.

Must it be conceded that Christians take leave of their genius in the inverse ratio of the distance they diverge from the forms of Catholicism? If they cannot conceive and execute edifices as well adapted to their form of worship, and decorate them as harmoniously as did the Catholics, then, it must be conceded, Protestantism is unfavorable to the development of art. Now, the truth is, Christianity is the *alma mater* of modern art. Aside from a few special symbols which serve to intensify the special dogma, the grand Christian temples of the middle ages are in spirit as much Protestant as Catholic. They are, pure and simple, the production of sensuous Christianity. They were conceived and executed when the whole Christian world nominally adhered to one creed; and hence the grandeur of their extent, the bold and lofty system of construction, and the sublime conception of their artistic decoration, the products of the concentrated energies of a whole nation centered upon a single subject. This concentrated religious zeal finally produced a mental development that desired to pass beyond the narrow limits which Catholicism had assigned to it; and the effort to attain mental emancipation, caused what is termed the Reformation.

The substance of all that can be said upon the subject of the Reformation is, that the concentrated power of the Romish hierarchy had outlived its usefulness; that, henceforth, Christianity was to be less sensuous, more practical, more individual in its character, and more solicitous for the universal good of all mankind. From the almost universal Catholic creed, the reformers went to the opposite extreme, and conceived creeds so definite and rigid, that it would appear every human soul must be formed in the same mould, to entertain the hope of salvation. But extremes usually work their own cure; and Protestantism, after passing through various phases, has finally arrived at universal toleration; and, in reaching that point, it repudiated all sensuous art, and in many instances still retains a prejudice against it.

Now, since there are no fears that Catholics and Protestants will ever be merged into one organization, I cannot see why the Catholic church should be permitted to monopolize what was purely the product of Christianity.

It is fit and proper to erect ornate structures for state or municipal purposes, or to construct magnificent dwellings to indicate the wealth and refinement of the private citizen; is it not proper that our sanctuaries for public worship be decorated as becomes the place and the object? As Protestant worship consists chiefly in seeing and hearing, the interiors of their churches should have no obstacles to interrupt the view, or break the sound from any person attending worship.

In construction they should be simple, yet grand, in effect; they will never require to be large, and therefore can readily be constructed without interior supports. As to style, there is but one that was purely the product of Christianity, and that is vulgarly called Gothic. It should have been called Christian; since the people known as the Goths had no more to do with the development of the pointed school of constructive art, than had the aborigines of America. Church architecture, with some professional architects, appears to be assuming a sort of "fashion" with very low walls, and frequently very low clear-stories, with enormous high roofs, and small windows, which frequently give to these structures the appearance of having been crushed into the earth by the weight of God's wrath, perhaps intended as a symbol of the Christian meekness of those who worship at its altars. Seriously, eccentricities of that, or of any kind, is not art, nor the evidence of genius or good taste; for the reason, they are not favorable to sound; they are not expressive of comfort; are poorly lighted and difficult to ventilate; nor can monstrosity of proportions be tortured into beauty. This sort of construction is purely exotic; it is not in harmony with our ideas; for the reason, it is retrogressive in its nature, in place of expansive and progressive, as are our national institutions. We are about entering upon the work of developing a national style of constructive art; and it appears to me that the only way we can arrive at noble results, is to make outline of plan and principles of construction to conform strictly to utility, and decorate the edifice in the manner that will distinctly, harmoniously, and pleasingly express the purpose it is designed to serve.

Then the language of art becomes clear, and a truthful record of the development of our national institutions; if art cannot do that, it has no special significance, and reflects little credit upon the nation or people who produce it. Our school of domestic constructive art is greatly in advance of our ecclesiastical, which may be attributed to two causes: first, the prejudice which the reformers conceived against the use of symbolic art; conceiving its excessive use to have been the cause, rather than the evidence, of the corruptions of the Romish church; and second, the comparative poverty of religious organizations, which poverty is no obstacle to growth of practical religious virtues, but a serious check upon the development of ecclesiastical art.

On the other hand, individual wealth is daily increasing, relatively, and hence the comparative rapid development of our domestic constructive art.

Yet all ornamentation of domestic constructive art is borrowed from sacred constructive art; and modern domestic art has derived its system of ornamentation from two sources: from the classic pagan, and from the pointed Christian; the former the physical sensuous, the latter the spiritual sensuous; the distinctive features of which have been described in preceding chapters, in their relations to religious organizations.

And as the two schools, in their origin, developed different forms to express different ideas and sentiments, so will the application of their decorative forms to domestic purposes express different ideas and different degrees of intelligence and cultivated taste; and in this, art remains true to itself. Now, since domestic art ministers more to our physical necessities than spiritual desires, it follows that its most appropriate forms of ornamentation are to be borrowed from the physically sensuous school.

The classic school of constructive art was secularized and utilized by the Romans, and has never regained its sacred character under the regime of Christianity, but has assumed a mixed form in certain localities; neither has the pointed or Gothic school been secularized, except in a mixed form. Hence, the purest domestic constructive art is that which adheres to the purer forms of classic art; as the purest forms of ecclesiastical art are those which adhere to the purer forms of the pointed Christian school of constructive art. Decorative art, in any and every form, is simply a symbolic language; and to perpetuate its true spirit, it is as essential to preserve the purity of the forms of the original schools, as it is to preserve the roots of the classic languages to preserve the purity of modern languages. This does not imply that it is essential to adhere to the temple forms with massive colonnades, since they were discarded by the Romans, but the gradual modification and refinement of details of ornamentation, to meet the necessities of the present system of domestic economy.

Classic art had its origin in cities and towns, has been chiefly employed in decorating town and city edifices, and has thus passed through various evolutions in the development of ancient and modern civilization.

Where culture has reached its highest development, there classic art has shed its refining influence; that is, it graces and refines the highest elements of physical and mental life; and as this condition can only be attained by intimate, unaffected, unostentatious social intercourse, hence it has received its highest modern development in the cities of Italy, France, and Germany. It has also obtained a firm footing in our own cities and towns; and if the desire for mere display does not finally supersede the love of elegant unostentatious refinement, its use will become more general, as the people become more cultivated and intelligent.

For suburban or country residences, the mixed styles are perhaps as appropriate as the pure Italian, as their indefinite and varied outlines harmonize with the surrounding scenery. The term, mixed styles, refers to those domestic structures known as the French chateau and English manor house, which have served as models for decorating many of our modern residences. They are termed mixed styles, for the reason, their original types were the feudal castles, which in their origin were plain massive structures, designed for shelter and fortification, in those rude ages when men were strangers to culture and refinement.

But during the development of agriculture, mechanics, and commerce, intelligence increased, domestic habits and customs underwent many changes, and the castle also passed through various modifications, borrowing its system of ornamentation from middle age art, until the revival of classic art, when the practice arose of modifying and enlarging the castle residence, and ornamenting by the introduction of classic details, which practice eventually developed those pseudo styles termed the "Elizabethan" in England, and the "Renaissance" in France.

Now, since the system of ornamentation of these mixed styles was derived from two distinct schools, the one whose principal lines were horizontal, and the other whose principal lines were vertical, it follows that there can never be that harmony in the lines, forms, and proportions of the system of ornamentation, that there is in a school where its lines are simple and harmonious. Consequently, the mixed styles are not capable of the same degree of simplicity, harmony, and refinement of expression as are the simple original schools.

Now, since the pointed Christian school has never been secularized to the same extent as has the classic, it follows that it is still the purest and most appropriate for ecclesiastical purposes in a Christian country. It is equally adapted to small as to large edifices, is susceptible of being simplified or highly elaborated, and is, therefore, capable of adaptation to the wants and desires of all Christian denominations.

On the other hand, classic art was secularized by the people who developed it; since they knew but the one style, they had to apply it to secular as well as sacred purposes. Its system of ornamentation has great elasticity. It has passed through many degrees of modification and refinement, and has thus become the available school for domestic purposes.

It is no detraction from American genius, nor circumscribing its sphere of action, to assert that it is not allotted to it to develop an original system of ornamentation, unless it originates a new system of religion.

And yet, all things considered, the field of constructive art is broader and more varied in our country than has heretofore appeared in any country.

We have a great number of Christian denominations; we have a greater number and variety of state, municipal, county, and town offices to provide accommodations for; and we have an infinitely greater variety of dwellings to provide,—from the palace to the cottage,—than can be found in any civilized country. And since our system of constructive art embraces so wide a practical field, it must of necessity, to a certain degree, become eclectic.

The genius for adaptation is second only to creative or inventive genius. It is semi-sensuous and semi-non-sensuous; the field of intellectual action is divided between the imagination and the experience. If semi-sensuous genius applies the materials it has in hand with true taste and sound judgment, we may yet hope for great and noble results.

SYNOPSIS.

HISTORY AND CONSTRUCTIVE ART: THEIR INTIMATE RELATIONS.

SYNOPSIS.

HISTORY AND CONSTRUCTIVE ART: THEIR INTIMATE RELATIONS.

The great mass of historical matter that has been preserved to the intelligent world since the commencement of the historic period, has become so unwieldy in its present form, that a general or special knowledge of history is impractical for the mass, and difficult as well as tedious for the student.

The significant events in history are so overlayed with sectarian prejudice, or obscured by the peculiar idiosyncrasies of historians, that their causes and effects seem to have been lost sight of, or treated as of secondary consideration.

It is true, the earliest authenic history represents man as in a different mental and physical condition from his present status; and from this fact, many historians ridicule what they please to term the bigotry and superstition of certain historic periods. I fail to see the justice or propriety of giving such slight consideration to certain periods of history, while so much importance is given to other periods.

The very idea of history pre-supposes change; and it is the difference in the physical, mental, and moral condition of man, that constitutes the true history, more than the time or space passed over during its occurrence. And it is this difference in the condition of man, in the various historic periods, that constitutes its value, as well as renders it interesting and instructive; and the comprehension of the causes of the differentiation at the different points upon the line of progress, must constitute the chief objects sought in historical investigation.

All that history can intelligibly impart to us is not so much the mere events, as it is the causes which have produced significant events, and what influences, if any, those events have exercised upon the future life of man. What our literature most needs is a complete unbroken history of the life of man, written in a liberal spirit, embracing all portions of his acts, whether relating to conquest, government, religion, art, literature, or philosophy. Such a work would doubtless be very difficult to compose; yet, as all the above-named subjects are embraced in history, and nearly simultaneous in their development, they have a direct relation to and influence upon their several developments.

A history written upon either of these subjects, without reference to the others, must necessarily be imperfect. As an instance, the history of the arts of a nation, considered independent of its religious and political institutions, conveys no higher ideas than mere abstract or ideal beauty; but when considered as an outgrowth of the moral and intellectual development of those institutions, conveys the very highest order of historic truth; and the same is true of all the special branches of human economy.

As history is the effect of organization, we perceive there are two subjects around which all organizations have centered, and from which all historic events diverge, as from two concentric curves; namely, religion and government. Of all the questions that have agitated the minds of men, these are the only two in which all minds have manifested a direct personal interest. The statesman, the philosopher, the poet, the artist, have labored to prove, or disprove, what to each seemed the great truths or fallacies embraced in these two grand subjects. Thus we shall see, if we minutely investigate any particular branch of social economy in any period of history, they all relate to these two subjects.

Therefore, it is clear, history should first be considered in its general character, although it may be the special branches that compose the general history. The special character of the arts, at any period of history, will mainly depend upon the system of religion; and the social, moral, and mental condition of the people will depend upon the special form of government. So gradual have been the changes in the mind of man upon the nature of these two grand subjects, they may be considered as differential merely, not radical. These differentiations arise from the development of the human mind; and man's acts upon his convictions of these varied and partial truths, are what constitute history, and a record of them is the evidence of human progress.

It is an error to suppose that conquest or annexation produces any sudden changes in the minds of men upon these subjects; if sudden changes appear to occur, it is because a nation or people are already divided in opinion upon these subjects; and internal weakness opens the way for external pressure, and conquest may follow.

In the amalgamation of two nations, a modification of the moral and mental condition of both takes place, and thus a new phenomenon in the life of man appears upon the stage of history.

No new elements of religion or of government that did not pertain to one or the other nation, may arise by the amalgamation, but there will be a modification of those that existed at the time of the amalgamation.

If both possess a developed school of arts, the amalgamation will develop a school different from either of the originals. The arts have generally been treated historically, as entirely independent of, and not necessarily connected with, other branches of social economy.

This is an erroneous view of the subject, as the monuments of art are the most ancient of all known records that furnish reliable information of the early history of man.

The nomenclature of art is as significant as that of language; it is much older, as the pictorial was the mode of expressing ideas anterior to the invention of characters expressing certain sounds. Since the invention of alphabets have come into general use, the pictorial has become nearly obsolete, and the public now conceive art to be the mere fancy of the individual, gotten up for the occasion, as the expression goes, by the mere fancy or ingenuity of the artist. It would be irrelevant to digress upon a philosophic dissertation of the mental organization of man to prove the necessity of his commencing at the pictorial, to arrive at the written, or sound-expressing characters, to convey his ideal emotions. It is sufficient for our purpose, that history proves that he did so commence his mental development. This, however, we may assert in addition: ideas are still conveyed in the pictorial mode, and the written is an abridgment of the process. In proof of this, we have only to call to mind the fact, that when language fails to convey our ideas, we resort to the figurative to illustrate them.

Therefore, the pictorial is the language in which nature addresses herself to man, and the language in which he comprehends and interprets her.

Consequently, art and civilization must have been simultaneous in their origin. Art emanates from man; he is the mould in which art is formed, and hence, clothes it in whatever is most expressive, and most pleasing to himself.

It is not to be inferred, however, that any special set or combination of forms will become a permanent standard; for, if that were so, it would be easy to fix and determine the form and outline of perfect beauty.

What, then, would become of art itself? Nothing but imitation would be left to it. What gives to art its highest significance, is its associations.

The monuments of art erected three thousand

years ago, are as true an abstract of the history at the time they were erected, as are those erected at present, or at any historic period. Therefore, the more history there is enacted, and the further its infancy recedes in the distance of time, the more interesting and instructive become the early monuments of art.

If we seek the higher elements of art, we must extend our vision beyond the precepts of books, or even beyond what may be derived from the study of the monuments of any one school, either ancient or modern. All art springs from our inner life, and the beauty it is striving to reveal is more special than general; for although the highest ideal conceptions may be realized under certain mental and physical conditions, yet the slightest change in these conditions will modify his ideal conceptions, and consequently enlarge the ideal of his art. Therefore, I cannot conceive of any law that governs the development of art, except those which govern the development of mind. In tracing the progress of history from its commencement to the present, we find three grand periods distinctly marked, namely, the ancient, the middle age, and the modern. There are, however, but two distinctly marked eras of civilization, the ancient and the modern. The middle period was merely the decay of the former, and the gradual development of the latter. As there are three periods of history, so there are three schools of constructive art: the horizontal, or classic; the round, or transition; and the vertical, or Christian. There are, however, but two original schools, the horizontal and the vertical. The round school was merely the transition from the horizontal to the vertical, or from pagan to Christian constructive art.

The decline of one original school and the rise of the other was caused by the decline of ancient, and the rise of modern civilization; or, more strictly speaking, the effect upon constructive art of the decay of the pagan, and the rise of the Christian systems of religion.

That this is a correct view of the subject, we have only to consider the development of art in connection with the progress of social economy.

While constructive art passes from the incipient state to the full development of a school or particular style, does man remain in the same primitive state? or does he also exhibit the phenomena of change? Is he better housed, better clothed? Has he better regulated religious and political institutions?

If these phenomena of change or progress in art and social institutions are simultaneous, we are forced to the conclusion that they are governed by the same laws of development.

One very important fact in connection with the subject should be considered; that is, the universal interest manifested in art in every period of history. Public sentiment has ever been its highest tribunal, and public approbation the highest reward of the artist. Therefore, the highest works of art are those most expressive of national genius. These alone are the works that survive the vicissitudes of time, and rise higher in the scale of immortality the longer they endure.

This, however, is more strictly true of ancient than of modern art; for the genius of humanity becomes more universal and less special the more it develops. And thus it is with art; the more schools there are developed, the more complicated, and, therefore, the less definite are its constructive forms.

For, as passion becomes subject to reason, art is subordinated to systems of religion and of government, which are but the ideal sentiments of a nation or race. Hence, we perceive the necessity for art to test its modern practice, by comparison with the original schools, as any lexicographer will testify to the necessity of referring to the classic to preserve the purity of modern language.

Therefore, no positive standard of positive forms can be decided upon, to test the merits of the different schools; for, as art can only be analyzed retrospectively, no just comparisons can be instituted until the grand ideal has reached its highest expression in artistic forms. Some theory or law may then be established, by the use of which the school may be imitated; but it is a fallacy to suppose that such laws were recognized in the infancy of the school.

We may as well assume the spontaneity of infancy to be subjected to mathematical rules, as to suppose art in its infancy is subjected to established laws.

It is equally fallacious to suppose that the laws of harmony and proportion that may be applicable to a past, are equally applicable to a present or a future school; for that would imply the immobility of mind as of art.

The extraordinary progress made in the last half century in the physical sciences, has given a stimulus to theorizing; and some claim to have made the discovery that the development of mind is subject to the same laws that govern the physical world.

Such a theory involves many serious and important questions. It subjects all ideal or mental impulse to the same laws that govern the movement of the body; and if pushed to its sequence, would draw Deity from nature, in place of nature from Deity.

We need not pursue the subject, as no benefit could be derived from it; but this may be said as relating to our subject: what has already been developed in mind or art, is equally true as that which remains to be developed; and it is equally true, that what has been developed, will never be developed again, which implies continuous change to be as much a law as continuous action.

I therefore leave this branch of the subject to those who have the taste and ability to pursue it.

This excessive proclivity to theorize is the grand obstacle in the way of the development of modern art. Antiquarians, in their admiration for classic art, have mistaken the letter for the spirit, and thus have assumed the forms and proportions of classic art to be the only true forms for all art, either ancient or modern.

On the other hand, others assume, that because the form and proportions of a Greek temple cannot be adapted to the use of a Protestant church or modern dwelling, they are no longer models of architectural excellence; and in like manner we might reject the entire schools of ancient art as unworthy our consideration.

Is it sufficient for our purpose to know that a

Greek temple is pronounced beautiful? Should we not know why it is beautiful? We should know whether it is the mere forms and proportions, or whether it is these combined with their symbolic sculpture, which give that expression of fitness of purpose which constitutes their exquisite beauty. The Greek temple without its symbolic forms of sculpture would have been as unmeaning to a Greek, as they are inappropriate to modern uses. The sculptures were the key to the mythical legend, and the Greek beheld in his temple the symbol of his faith and the record of his history. The mythical has passed into written history; and hence, art is no longer subjected to a symbolized mythology, but is guided by man's rational belief and moral and social condition.

The physical beauty of art, and its forms of geometry, remain substantially the same; the laws of harmony, of outline, of form, and proportions of quantities, remain the same as developed in the Greek temples; yet the ideal in the mind of man cannot be reduced to a positive standard, for the reason that function is perpetual.

The two radical ideas that man has conceived upon the nature and attributes of Deity, has developed two radical elements in art; and aside from these, I know of nothing that has developed original elements in constructive art.

The pagan idea of Deity was man deified, and men were his children. Consequently, there is nothing above the physical in pagan art. When, however, man came to conceive Deity as a spiritual being, existing above physical nature, then it was that physical forms were made to express physical ideas; and hence came Christian art to be radically different in its construction and decoration from the pagan. Secular art is not independent of sacred, but holds the same relations to the sacred, as secular institutions do to religious institutions.

There is nothing noble, elevating, or inspiring in the contemplation of secular, when compared with sacred art, yet the secular has become of more importance than even the sacred.

What is the consequence? Art, as all admit, is on the decline; whereas it should be in the ascendant. We see this manifest in various ways.

First, men no longer consider God's holy temple as the proper receptacle for the spontaneous products of man's loftiest emotions, in the product of sacred or symbolic art. They find more fitting subjects for their aspirations in decorating their own temporal abiding-places. I am led to speak thus freely, as I feel my duty to the subject requires that I should expose fallacies, as well as point out truths.

A private residence fashioned in correct taste, and in keeping with the fortune of the owner, may be art, if the idea expressed be convenience, domestic ease, and unostentatious refinement; for such are the virtues of private life in a Christian country.

These facts should be understood by the critic as well as the artist; for no person is competent to pass judgment upon a work of art, until he is familiar with this much of its elements. Two ideas only are present in the mind of the uneducated, while contemplating a work of art; namely, sublimity and beauty. All compound ideas are derived from their practical application to some special subject or object. A school of art is the development of a grand idea to its highest expression, in forms and colors, of the physical and mental qualities. All ideas, however, when first presented to the mind, are crude and undeveloped; and however sublime or beautiful may be their conception, to embody them in a work of art will depend upon a knowledge of forms and colors. A knowledge of the language of these forms and colors, and a command of their mechanical execution, are what make the artist; one other quality is wanting to make the great artist, namely, a vivid and creative imagination.

The history of constructive art clearly illustrates the homogeneity of ideas in their nascent state; and the eras of the schools show their development to be the passing from homogeneity to heterogeneity, as the earliest specimens of each school were more massive and simple in detail, than were the later works. It is beyond question, that modern constructive art derives its forms and its ideas of proportion from the classic schools. The ancients conceived Deity as a physical force, and, hence, very naturally personated him in natural forms. This was clearly illustrated in their temples, and especially in the Greek, where we see each column in the peristyle formed to express the physical powers and masculine beauty of the god to whom the temple was dedicated. On its friezes were sculptured, in symbolic figures, his legendary history; and in the tympanum was placed the scene of his apotheosis. Yet this concentration of ideas upon the individual, with no higher conception than the physical, at once limited the sphere of art. Yet, while it limited its sphere of action, it tended to perfection of forms and proportions, and finally culminated in that model of form, the Parthenon.

The measure of Greek art was therefore complete; yet art itself was in no way complete in its development, as another element of art yet remained to be developed, the spiritual. The transition was neither sudden nor violent, but steady and irresistible.

At the perfection of physical form, life only was wanting; and the robing of physical forms with a spiritual expression, emancipated art from the restraints that an arbitrary law of harmony and proportion had thrown around it, and hence enlarged its sphere of action.

This new element of art, however, did not create new forms, since it cannot be claimed for middle age or modern art that they contain more, or different, geometrical forms from the classic. The difference in the schools consists in the different combination of forms and proportions of parts to each other. Religion and government were the grand leading ideas of the ancient, as of the modern world; and the difference in belief and practice upon these grand leading ideas, has developed a differentiated civilization, which has caused the difference in construction and ornamentation of the different schools of constructive art. It was the Greek system of mythology that developed, in such splendor and perfection, the school of physical beauty called the classic; and it was Christian spiritualism that produced that expansive and aspiring school, falsely called the Gothic. Since it was purely Christian in its origin, it should be so called.

These are the only schools that contain radically distinct elements of construction and ornamentation; all other schools are the modification, or amalgamation, of these two. The arch, which is the most useful, as well as one of the grandest features in the building art, is the connecting link between the pagan classic and Christian spiritual schools.

Its base rests upon the sepulchre of the post and lintel system; and upon its apex stands, in all its lofty and aspiring grandeur, the vertical system of construction. The constructive principles of the post and lintel system were inadequate to meet the demands of the expansive elements of Roman civilization.

The thirst for power and dominion gave an expansiveness to Roman mind that could not be controlled by that mere refinement of physical beauty, that so captivated and enslaved the Greek.

Neither was Roman art confined so exclusively

to temple building, as was the Greek. Roman art, therefore, became gradually secularized; the growth of the empire developed wealth and commerce, which necessitated the construction of a class of buildings before unknown.

As the Romans extended their conquests, their love of power increased, and their veneration for sacred things gradually diminished, until their arts presented more of a secular than a sacred character.

In this condition was pagan art, when Christianity came before the world to teach salvation to all men through faith and repentance. The first places for public worship selected by the Christians, were a class of buildings entirely secular in their character. They were doubtlessly chosen for their convenience, while they were less repulsive to the Christian than were those temples consecrated to the worship of the pagan deities.

The basilicas, which were the first places selected for Christian worship, were originally erected for mercantile purposes; yet so well adapted were they, that they became the models for the construction of all early Christian churches.

One insurmountable obstacle to the use of the temple, was its unfitness, in construction and internal arrangement, for Christian worship.

Pagan temples were erected chiefly for external effect, since the interiors were used for little else than to place the statue of the deity to whom the temple was dedicated, and to receive its votive offerings. They had not even windows to admit air and light. The larger class were lighted by omitting a portion of the roof. Such a class of buildings could not have been easily converted into Christian churches, had there been no other obstacles in the way of their adoption. The elements of the two religions were too antagonistic to permit of so near an approach to a mutual recognition, as to consent to worship in the same edifice. Fortunate, doubtless, it was for Christianity that such was the case.

It had been the practice of the Romans to admit into the Pantheon every new or strange god, with each accession of conquest; and in like manner did they propose to place the God of the Christian; but from this proposition they shrank as from the embrace of a monster.

The pagan deities, although obsolete in the minds of the majority of their votaries, still held the sacred place in the state; yet they were in the keeping of the hypocritical formalist, who was elevated to high places by his professions of reverence for the gods and love for the state, who had made both the instruments to minister to his ambition, until every institution, either sacred or profane, was prostituted by fraud, licentiousness, and oppression.

The poor and oppressed had never found protection, nor but a negative consolation, in their devotions to the pagan religion; and as the genius of humanity is ever quickened by its own misfortunes, it was to this class that Christianity first addressed itself; and were there no higher evidences, this alone would be ample to prove its humane principles.

However divine the source from whence Christianity may have emanated, or however convincing may have been its great truths to the minds of its first converts, its mission was twofold: to eradicate error, and implant truth. Whatever virtues there may have been in pagan institutions in their infancy or maturity, the progress of society had exceeded the bounds of their moral ethics; to the well-informed, the whole system had become a mockery. Yet, it is true, all the machinery of society was based upon pagan ethics; but they no longer possessed the cohesive force necessary to hold its institutions together; and every pillar in the fabric was crumbling under the accumulated weight of infidelity and licentiousness.

The grand idea of pagan religion was hero-worship; the great virtue of the individual, therefore, was personal bravery, or heroic deeds.

Consequently, conquest became the grand object of the state; and to such an extent had this idea been carried by the Romans, that internal weakness and consequent exhaustion could no longer resist the external pressure of its overgrown provinces, and Rome sank under the accumulated weight of her own heroic deeds. The legions that once shook the earth as they filed out of the gates of the "Eternal City," were now flying before the superior prowess of the victorious barbarians. Her legislative halls, where once her pro-consuls dictated laws to the world, now re-echoed the voice of the voluptuous and degenerate Roman, upon whose shoulders had descended, with apparent grace and ease, the mantle of despotism.

The magistrates no longer exercised the authority of censors of the people; public morals and private virtue had sunk too low for regeneration; their ethical system was exhausted, and public faith was dead.

In the midst of these dissolving elements, Christianity was first planted in the thin soil of public virtue that still remained exposed to the light. Yet it had developed no arts of its own; and, consequently, was at first compelled to adopt so much of pagan arts as was essential to self-preservation. It was the subordination of art and literature to luxury and licentiousness, that prolonged the existence of paganism in the midst of the youthful and growing institutions of Christianity.

Yet, in proportion as pagan institutions declined,

Christian institutions increased in numbers and influence, until they became the possessors of literature and art.

One pagan custom, however, the Christians retained: that of consecrating certain places to the special use and offices of the church. Whether the early Christians believed in or clearly comprehended the sublime idea of the impartial ubiquity of God, or the equitable omnipresence of the Redeemer, they countenanced the idea of the superior sanctity of certain places, and consecrated them to the special offices of their religious organizations. This not merely gave protection to their institutions, but was the most effective means of supplanting the pagan with the Christian worship; since they chose as places for worship, structures entirely secular, and consecrated them to the worship of the true God. This was the first step toward the development of a new school of art; what had before been merely secular, now became sacred; and what had been sacred, now became obselete, as a religious idea.

Roman art had reached its culminating point at

the advent of Christianity; and when Christians were first permitted by imperial authority to worship in public, it was rapidly declining; nor did the change in the policy of the government arrest its downward tendency; for the reason, all the social organizations of the empire, were rapidly disintegrating. The decline of the empire may be attributed to the decay of Roman military supremacy; her greatness was the result of conquest, more than of self-culture.

Her gods, her arts, and her literature, were borrowed from Etruria, Greece, and Egypt; and every conquered province furnished its quota of works of art, merchandise, captives, and precious jewels, to adorn the triumph of the conqueror, replenish the treasury, and add new specimens of art to the galleries of the imperial city. And what had she furnished in return? A standing army to be fed and clothed, and the avarice of a military governor to be gratified.

The cause of the decline of Roman institutions has its explanation in the narrow and illiberal policy upon which they were founded. Nor did the policy of the later emperors succeed in consolidating into one people the heterogeneous mass of centuries of conquests. Confederation and rebellion to regain personal or national independence, was almost constant. This was the chief cause of the change from a republic to an empire. The change effected a temporary submission, but it failed to accomplish its purpose, since it could neither command the love nor respect of the conquered; and when the emperors felt the scepter gradually but steadily sliding from their grasp, they attempted to create a representative government, but did not succeed.

Personal independence was what each city or confederacy desired; and at the final extinction of the empire, they regained their independent condition.

This want of sympathy and unity of purpose finally undermined the central power, and caused the decline of literature and art, as well as government.

Christianity alone remained the future hope and regenerator of society. But this was a work for centuries of time to accomplish; and when the work of regeneration did really commence, it began with a new development of society and of art.

Christian ethics and the feudal system were the elements upon which the new society founded its organizations. When the barbaric invasions ceased, society began to assume a more staple form under the feudal system. Feudalism in its infancy was merely an aggregation of petty communities, under the control of a single individual; all, however, acknowledging the Christian church as the supreme head. The church thus became the centre of the new order of society. Wherever the feudal princes established their abode, they built a fortified residence, or castle, and surrounded it with the tenements of their vassals. In the midst of this isolated community, the church erected the house of prayer. Nor did it hesitate to become both lord and vassal, thus giving aid and support to establishing order in society, even upon this narrow basis.

It was under the feudal system that the rights of women were first conceded; the feudal lord was the first public personage who, from necessity or choice, made his wife his chief social companion. The church had also placed woman on an equality with man, as regards her future destiny. Here, then, we have the type of modern social and religious institutions.

This was the heroic age of modern, as the Greek legendary was that of ancient civilization. At this period, the church and people were one in sympathy and impulse. The church had risen from the people, and in the plenitude of her power she opened the wide portals of her sanctuaries as an asylum to the poor and the oppressed.

This zeal and enthusiasm, this love to God and love to man, which was the basis of the early Christian church, was the secret passion that regenerated society and art.

All pagan institutions and arts were now dissolved into Christian elements.

The temple which formerly contained but the statue of the pagan deity, had expanded into the broad-aisled cathedral, the sanctuary of the faithful, filled with the penitents, where the altar of the Lord is raised, as a symbol of his invisible presence.

In this work of regeneration, the elements of art have been transposed; the peristyle of columns has become attached buttresses; the straight lintel has been superseded by the round or pointed arch; buildings erected for external effect have given place to those for internal use; sculpture, that so delighted to personate physical beauty, has given place to painting, which, in the spirit of Christian asceticism, devotes itself to the agonies of the soul, in its thirst for immortality.

One element was now wanting to develop the arts of the Christian church to a new and independent school, and that was action. The mental activity of the church had only stimulated its more devout followers to an ascetic life, thus leaving the social organizations to perish for want of active elements. An event finally occurred that infused new life and energy into society; and that was the Crusades. The slumbering energies of humanity answered promptly to the call to go forth in the name of the Lord, and of mother church, to smite with the sword the accursed infidel who had desecrated the Holy Sepulchre, and driven from the holy places the pious pilgrims. No event in modern history stands out in such bold relief, has left such indelible impressions, or wrought such changes in the forms of society, upon which there has been expressed such laudatory and denunciatory opinions, as upon the subject of the Crusades. They have generally been considered as an accidental result, caused by the recitals of pilgrims returning from the Holy Land, and the preaching of Peter the Hermit, in his appeals to the religious enthusiasm of an ignorant populace. A careful inquiry into the history of the times in which they occurred, will attribute their origin to a very different cause.

However general may have been the practice of performing pilgrimages in the tenth and eleventh centuries, the custom cannot be said to have originated with Christians, but must be considered as belonging to the universal religion of man. Neither is the practice to be so hastily condemned, as it often has been by historians and theologians;

for it is but rational to suppose that humanity then, as now, was subject to the same weaknesses, sympathies, passions, and emotions. If the superior intelligence of the nineteenth century has taught men to comprehend the sublime idea of the impartial ubiquity of God, yet it may consistently be inferred that a lack of a proper comprehension of those great elements of Deity very naturally led the early Christians to believe in the superior sanctity of those places associated with the life and death of the Saviour. The difference in the belief of the eleventh and nineteenth centuries, is one of degree more than of quality.

Christianity had touched the hearts of men, if it had not conveyed sufficient light of reason to check the religious enthusiasm; and when the appeal was made to defend the Holy Sepulchre, the church did not lack for champions.

Nobles, priests, and people assumed the badge of the red cross, and took their way to the scene of future contest. Some sold their patrimonial estates, others mortgaged their inheritances and manumitted their vassals, that they might join in the great struggle between Christianity and Islamism. The monks came forth from their retirement, and formed themselves into military orders, to fight under the banners of the cross; the Pope exhorted the faithful to enlist in the cause, and gave them his blessing.

To such an extent did the enthusiasm prevail, and so reckless of life and consequences were the leaders of these hordes of enthusiasts, that their wanderings might have been traced by the bones of the victims that perished upon the way, from the banks of the Rhine to the very walls of Jerusalem.

This universal movement of humanity gave a new impetus to its energies, increased the power and wealth of the church, and the religious enthusiasm and romance consequent upon these movements, and gave a poetic and artistic turn to intellectual action.

From these sources of mental enthusiasm and ideal creations, sprung as by magic that spiritualized ideal school of constructive art, whose monuments still rest in repose in central and western Europe.

The school took its rise in the heart of France, where the crusaders had been most numerous and most enthusiastic, and there it continued to flourish with a profuse and luxuriant growth. Its spires, pinnacles, and flying buttresses shot upward like magic, while the lofty vaults of the naves and aisles, with their supports of slender, clustered pillars, seemed to bid defiance to all the before known laws of construction.

The decline of this school was as rapid as its growth. Founded, doubtless, as it was, in the zeal and enthusiasm of Christianity in the twelfth century, in its infancy it had no positive laws of proportion, nor developed system of ornamentation, but was the pure offspring of the imagination. In its middle life, however, it began to adopt mathematical rules for proportions and forms, which gradually became more arbitrary, until the school culminated in a series of mathematical problems, illustrated by geometrical forms.

The French historian, Michelet, asserts Gothic architecture to be purely the offspring of the imagination, yet insists it was developed under a regular.law, which culminated in the cathedral of Cologne. His theory is: every Gothic edifice has its numerical standard, which, with its sub-divisions and multipliers, is the guiding measure of the whole structure. Some such theory applied to the later works of this school may prove true, as it would when applied to the later works in any school; yet that such, or any, positive laws govern in the infancy of their development, I believe to be fallacious.

The imagination of youth is more vivid than in middle or old age; and although genius may retain the mind in that solvent state that is ever susceptible to new impressions, yet method is essential to practical development; and hence it follows, the more the imagination is subjected to the practical, the more it relies upon reflection, and the law of reflection is the law of numbers.

As art is entirely human in its origin, all its works, past or present, must be referred to the sentiments and passions of man. It is therefore subject to the same laws as govern the development of the human mind, and its merits or demerits must be determined by the same court that sits in judgment upon man's past history. Memory and reflection are the faculties brought into action when philosophy commences its labors, and the legitimate subjects in connection with art are the past acts of man, their causes and effects. It neither creates nor destroys, but reduces the imaginative to the practical; art alone creates; philosophy sits in judgment upon the causes and necessities of its creations.

Yet, as the aspirations and hopes of man are ever changing, so will the products of art change with every new demand made upon it. This constant change in the external features of art does not prove the past schools to be fallacious to-day, but everlasting truths of the past, so to remain as long as their monuments endure.

The realization of a grand idea prepares mankind to pass on to the development of other ideas; and the same is true of art. The post and lintel style of the Greeks prepared the way for the pier and arch style of the Romans; and the pier and arch style prepared the way for the buttress, pointed arch, and pinnacle style of the Christians. Thus we perceive there has been a regular movement from one mode of construction to the reverse, by successive developments of varied ideas. Each in its turn has been realized by a series of art crystallizations, while the genius of humanity remained in solution, ever susceptible to new impressions.

These poetic forms of art in the infancy of a school, are purely ideal creations; but as the grand idea is developed with successive series, form itself develops the actual by its subordination to purposes of utility. Art, consequently, becomes comparatively stationary, as utility supersedes the imaginative.

A mere repetition of mathematical forms is a retrograde movement, since a multiplication of the same forms is but an aggregation of the material, or merely mechanical; and when art falls into this material condition, it must so remain until some radical movement takes place either in religion or social organizations; when the iconoclast, breaking the fetters that confined genius, opens a new field for the imagination, by creating the necessity for new arrangements of construction, thus necessitating new combinations of ornamentation.

This remodeling of old forms to meet the exigencies of a new order of things, is clearly exemplified in the revival of classic art in the fourteenth century. The revival commenced in Italy; and it is proper to state, the Gothic or vertical style had never flourished in its purity in Italy. From the decline of the Roman to the revival of the classic, Italian art had remained in that degraded state where classic forms had been tortured into all conceivable fantastic shapes, to give an expression to Christian esthetics, with partial success. As compared with the pointed, the classic is immeasurably below, both in artistic expression and fitness of purpose, for Christian ecclesiastical edifices; for, it must be remembered, the classic was conceived and executed for external effect, while the pointed had its inception and development for internal use; and so long as Christian churches continue to be erected for the purpose of assembling in, in place of outwardly gazing upon, so long will the pointed continue to be the most fit and appropriate style for Christian churches.

The classic has continued to be the style of the Catholic church in Italy from the introduction of Christianity to the present; and it is a question whether the Italians have, or ever had, that elevated and spiritual conception of Christianity that has influenced the northern and western nations of Europe. Certain it is, their progress has been marked chiefly by the increase of the physical machinery of their established church.

M. Taine, a recent French essayist, says of St. Peter's, of Rome, and the Cathedral of Florence, "They are the works of pagans in fear of damnation."

The revival of classic art in Italy was caused by the rise of commerce, the rise and growth of free cities, and the increase of wealth and influence of the middle class, more than by any special movement of religious organizations. Consequently, it was more secular than ecclesiastical in its character; and this is true of the revival of the arts (as the term is) in France and England.

The decay of the power of the feudal barons, as modern civilization was developed, gradually transformed the feudal castle into the modern country villa; and the consolidation of the power of the monarchies built up a series of palaces that gave character and patronage to art.

The Reformation had also given rise to a new class of ecclesiastical structures, which were equally well adapted for religious purposes. The reformers, however, were as bigoted in their views of art as of religion; and, in the obtuseness of their vision, they fancied they saw in those splendid monuments of art only the evidence of corruption, which had grown out of the use and abuse of power; and they sought to reform those abuses by destroying those monuments of art, which were but the evidences of the zeal and enthusiasm of a past age.

Grant that the arts may have aided in the abuses and impositions of the Romish church, yet the reformers went to the opposite extreme, by not admitting a decent respect to be paid to the house of God, but denying the admission of appropriate symbols of that religion to whose use it was consecrated.

As knowledge became disseminated, this Puritan spirit gradually subsided; but the spirit of Christian art had departed, and the revival of classic art and literature had disseminated an affectation of taste that was neither adapted to modern institutions, nor in harmony with the national genius. This is especially true of the introduction of purely Grecian models, either for domestic or ecclesiastical purposes.

The genius of the age was experimental, not imaginative; and it was not in the power of the antiquarian or man of science to adapt Grecian models to the wants of modern institutions.

Europe and America tried the experiment, with about equal success. There was, however, a seeming necessity on the part of Americans that they should borrow from some source what they had neither inherited in their adopted country, nor had the privilege of beholding; namely, such models of the arts as modern civilization had developed. Europe has a regular succession of monuments, that were erected at each stage of development; America has nothing of the kind.

The Puritan fathers had brought civilization with them as it then existed in Europe; but they planted it in the wilderness, where not a trace of a previous civilized state then existed. Religious and political liberty was the grand object sought by our Pilgrim fathers in immigrating to America. The Reformation, as it is termed, was more negative than positive in its character, since its object was to reform old and decrepit institutions, rather than to supersede them with new.

This contest finally centered upon a struggle for the superiority of individual opinion, especially upon the matter of religious creeds, each sect contending for the superiority of its own faith.

Fortunately, however, these negative ideas have nearly passed, and the fruits of the contests are religious freedom and toleration. That there may be, as there surely is, an honest difference of opinion upon many minor points of practical Christianity, every candid mind now concedes; and this is the most that could be accomplished by a religious reformation.

As all high art emanates from the religious emotions, in this divided state of religious worship, art accommodates itself to the demands made upon it; and if it is confined to smaller structures, there are a greater number and variety of uses, and, consequently, a more varied system of construction and ornamentation. All things considered, the field of constructive art is as wide to-day as it was when it was the monopoly of a single religious institution; its power is modified, while its variety is multiplied.

Art can, and ought to be, as expressive to-day for Protestants, as it has been in the past for pagans or Christians.

There is the same unity of spirit in their organizations and public worship; but the misfortune is, when any artistic effort is made, they copy the letter, rather than the spirit of the arts of the past. They aim to make a Protestant church a Romish cathedral, with its nave, aisles, and transepts, in place of a single unobstructed nave, where all may see and hear the service. These false practices have produced a false style of art, and, unless corrected, will prevent the development of an American, or Protestant, style of constructive art; which would be new constructive elements, and new combinations of ornaments, more than the creation of new forms.

Why should not America produce a style of art as purely her own as are her social institutions? Why should not Protestants build edifices suited to their wants, without regard to what has been the practice of others? As art is purely human in its origin, it is limited in its capacity precisely as man is limited: it can be pagan or Christian, Catholic or Protestant; and in these changes of purpose, it exhibits no more radical elements than does man in creating their necessity.

www.ingramcontent.com/pod-product-compliance
Lightning Source LLC
LaVergne TN
LVHW020243110826
845151LV00003B/1015
* 9 7 8 1 4 2 5 5 2 8 9 5 9 *